COMFORT
IS AN
OLD BARN

Also from Islandport Press

Mountain Girl
Marilyn Moss Rockefeller

And Poison Fell from the Sky
MarieThérèse Martin

Bald Eagles, Bear Cubs and Hermit Bill
Ron Joseph

Moon in Full
Marpheen Chann

The Ghosts of Walter Crockett
W. Edward Crockett

Dear Maine
Morgan Rielly and Reza Jalali

Take it Easy
John Duncan

Whatever it Takes
May Davidson

Hauling by Hand
Dean Lawrence Lunt

COMFORT IS AN OLD BARN

Stories from the Heart of Maine

Amy Calder

ISLANDPORT PRESS

ISLANDPORT PRESS

Islandport Press
P.O. Box 10
Yarmouth, Maine 04096
www.islandportpress.com
info@islandportpress.com

First Edition: January 2023
Printed in the United States of America.
All photographs, unless otherwise noted, courtesy of Amy Calder.
Cover Photo by Algis Kemezys

ISBN: 978-1-952143-47-2
Ebook ISBN: 978-1-952143-58-8
Library of Congress Control Number: 2022942585

Dean L. Lunt | Editor-in-Chief, Publisher
Emily A. Lunt | Book Designer

For my husband, Phil Norvish—
always my best critic.

TABLE OF CONTENTS

On the Beat

The People I Meet

Epilogue

Author's Note

I grew up in the late fifties, sixties, and early seventies in rural Skowhegan, the youngest in a brood of seven imaginative, adventurous, and sometimes unruly kids. I scoured the nearby woods and fields; built boats, cabins, and tree houses; rode horses; and tore around the back lot in my brothers' old cars. We climbed trees, fished, swam, and explored old barns. To this day, I can't pass a barn without recalling the scent of hay and the comfort I felt while lazing around in one as a spring rain pounded the roof.

A central Maine childhood also afforded me the opportunity to meet many characters, and I couldn't get enough of the stories they told. I think the experience served to inform my love of telling others' stories as I grew older.

My father, Edwin Ross Calder, was a traveling salesman during my early life, although he had served with the U.S. Navy in the South Pacific during World War II. Later, he worked for the Kennebec Log Driving Company, which moved pulpwood south from Moosehead down the river, stopping in 1976 when the log drives ended. He was also an avid golfer. He and my mother—Frances Emma Rowell Calder, a registered nurse who trained at what is now Maine Medical Center in Portland—bought a large house on about thirty acres in Skowhegan in 1958 when I was two, and we moved there from Norridgewock. My siblings, Richard—the oldest at nine years older than I—Katherine, David, Matthew, Laura, and Jane, would later

Me and my siblings in 1956. (L to R): Matthew, David, me, Richard, Jane, Katherine, and Laura.

become teachers, construction workers, and farmers. David, who also worked on the log drive, has written, composed the music for, sang, and recorded songs about the last log drive on the Kennebec.

Our mother had a keen sense of humor, played the piano and clarinet, and was a terrific baker. My father, who studied at what was then the Portland School of Fine & Applied Art, was a talented artist. They lived in their Skowhegan house until they died, both at ninety-two, in 2010 and 2015, respectively.

I attended North Elementary School, Margaret Chase Smith School, Skowhegan Junior High School, and finally Skowhegan Area High School, from which I graduated in 1974. While a teenager, I struck a deal with my mother—I could use the family car on weekends as long as I fetched her at midnight from her late shift at the local hospital. It is one of my favorite memories. Sometimes, I had to stay at the hospital until the wee hours of the morning because the emergency room where she worked got so busy—and often, she was the only person on duty.

I loved sitting in the waiting room watching all the characters come and go (some, inebriated), all with different ailments or complaints. I listened to their stories and was fascinated by their lives. I relished being asked to help at times. A doctor once hauled me into a treatment room (I was about sixteen) to help with two crash victims whose car had gone off a bridge in Solon. He handed me a pair of scissors and ordered me to cut their clothes off so he could tend to their wounds.

After high school, I attended the University of Hartford in West Hartford, Connecticut, majoring in English. I also took journalism classes and worked as a reporter and arts editor at the student newspaper. After earning my bachelor's degree, I studied education at University of Massachusetts at Amherst for a full year, including the summer. I student-taught at Frontier Regional High School in South Deerfield, Massachusetts, and got my certification to teach secondary English in the Commonwealth of Massachusetts, but when it was time to launch a teaching career, I realized journalism was where I really belonged.

I began writing for the *Morning Sentinel* in Waterville in 1988, more than thirty-four years ago, and I have never left. I love it too much. While my beat is Waterville city government, education, crime, economic development, and so on, I

My father and mother in 1998.

3

also get to cover all sorts of other events, such as fires, accidents, and murders.

Working as a news reporter for more than three decades has afforded me plenty of opportunities to write about people and their trials, plights, tragedies, and joys. I feel fortunate to have been allowed into their lives to hear their stories and retell them.

Some fourteen years ago, I was asked to start writing a weekly human interest column called "Reporting Aside." I decided I would steer away from hard news in the column and instead feature central Mainers doing interesting things, tell some stories about my childhood, and once in a while, offer my opinion if I felt strongly enough about something. The column work led me down a path I never imagined I would relish so much. It gave me the opportunity to spread my wings a bit from the who, what, when, where, and why of news writing, be creative, and dig a bit into my past. It also gave me the freedom, when ideas came slowly, to hop in my car and drive around until I found interesting people willing to tell me their stories. And everyone, I learned, has them.

Amy Calder
Waterville, Maine
January 2023

GROWING UP

Comfort is an Old Barn

I hate seeing old barns sagging and leaning from the weight of time and aging timbers.

Many years ago, as I traveled around central Maine chasing stories, I'd make mental notes of all those old barns I saw, with the intention of one day photographing them and collecting the images in a book. The barns were so beautiful, their gray shingles weathered from sun, rain, and snow. I knew that one day they'd fall away and disappear, and we'd never see them again. I regret that I never photographed them as planned.

The old barns of Maine carry lots of stories, hold many memories, and remind us of the sweetness of rural life. There's something exquisite about an old barn standing there in a field, a remnant from a time when farmers tossed hay into wagons with pitchforks on a hot summer day, the scent of fresh hay wafting through the air.

Barns were an integral part of my youth; I can't dream about my past without remembering those magnificent structures where horses stomped around in their stalls, eyeing us curiously as we approached, and cows chewed on feed. The scent of hay was intoxicating. My friends and I would climb up into the haylofts and meander through the bales, hold conferences, and take turns jumping off into hay mounds below.

Barns were great napping places—quiet, comfortable, and safe.

It was never a wasted day, spending time in a barn with the animals—feeding, washing, and brushing a horse; shoveling manure and spreading a fresh bed of straw; or merely sitting on a bucket, watching someone else do it. Sweeping away errant chaff from old barn boards, polishing a saddle, organizing bits and bridles on posts: it was all good work, satisfying work.

I got to thinking about those barns one day while attempting to tidy up and organize my mother's barn—the barn I spent many days in as a youth. I know every nook and cranny of that old structure, every beam, peg, and hole in the floorboards. The barn still visits my dreams, albeit it has been decades since I played there.

As children, we staged plays and dance recitals in the second-floor loft, assigning seats below to the mothers of the neighborhood kids who performed there. We played house, hospital, hide-and-seek, and storekeeper in the barn, climbing deftly up and down beams like monkeys, never needing a ladder. We had hiding places, cubbyholes, and special rooms designated for club meetings. The barn kept our secrets.

My friend Terri got the nickname "Hayseed" from spending so much time there. It was our castle, the place we ran to when a summer shower struck; it was a daylong refuge during a good, hard rain. There's nothing so sweet as sitting just inside the open front door of a barn during a downpour, watching the world outside from that safe, dry, contemplative place.

There's comfort to be found from being inside a barn—a sense of being grounded.

Although we sold the family property in Skowhegan after my mother died on New Year's Day in 2015, I still dream about the old barn where I spent so many happy hours. In those modern dreams, I climb to the second-floor loft where an ancient, dusty canoe lies across the floorboards, chipped cups and saucers we used to play house are scattered about, boxes of discarded books and other debris are stacked in corners, and barn swallows are swooping in and out of a broken window at the roof's peak.

Balancing as if on a tightrope, I step across a wooden plank perched over an open chicken coop below. Although the plank bows in the middle, I never fall in.

Those dreams, I think, portend that all is well, despite what we have lost to time. In those old barns, we learned, discovered, imagined, dreamed fearlessly—and prevailed.

Skowhegan in the 1960's

One quiet Monday after Christmas, we older employees in the *Morning Sentinel* newsroom got to talking about what it was like growing up in central Maine during the sixties. No question, it was a lot different than it is today.

My family lived in the country, where houses were separated by fields, woods, and pastures. My brothers and sisters and I could walk to and from our friends' houses in the dark, late at night, never once worrying that someone might kidnap or kill us. Our parents left us in the car with the doors unlocked when they went into a store. The thought that someone might steal us never crossed their radar. We never locked our house doors at night, and we didn't worry about protecting ourselves with guns. If we did have guns, they were for hunting.

Kids didn't go to school worrying about getting shot nor did they take part in active shooter drills. Our drills were more global in scope—to prepare for a nuclear bomb attack. We were told to duck under our desks and put our heads down. At the time, I didn't really understand what it all meant but dutifully followed instructions.

The house in Skowhegan where I grew up.

During summer, our daily itinerary wasn't carefully planned in advance unless we were celebrating a holiday or taking a family road trip. We'd get up each morning and race out the door toward whatever adventures we could dream up—roaming the woods and fields, building tree houses, swimming, fishing, or playing baseball.

My family—my mother, my father, and their seven children—lived about two miles from downtown Skowhegan in an old ten-room farmhouse that my father painted yellow with light blue shutters. We owned a huge field and acres of woods behind our house where we were free to roam without supervision. Our house was surrounded by large lawns and shaded by maple, oak, and pine trees. Lilac bushes, roses, and lilies all added beauty and color to the property, and my father kept a big garden that provided us with vegetables to eat all year long. While the mile-long road to our house was flat, it intersected with others that led out to rolling hills, pastures, hayfields, woods, and streams.

My siblings and I didn't watch television during the day, and, of course, there were no cell phones or computers. In our house, we had a party line telephone, which meant multiple families shared the same telephone line. When we picked up the phone receiver to make a call, sometimes one of our neighbors would already be talking to someone, so we would hang up and wait until they were done.

We read the daily newspaper—the *Morning Sentinel*, of course—and my sisters Jane and Laura and I loved to read Nancy Drew novels. We huddled around the forced air furnace on the floor at the foot of the stairs on cold winter mornings reading classics we were assigned in school, such as *Great Expectations, Huckleberry Finn,* and *A Tale of Two Cities.* But we also loved reading comic books featuring characters like Dick Tracy and Archie and Veronica or whatever else we could find around the house. When we were bored, we read my mother's nursing books, which she stored in her bedroom closet. When she was out of the house, we'd retrieve those books and scare ourselves out of our wits looking at all the pictures of skin diseases, deformities, and other maladies.

We didn't go to the movie theater often, but when we did, it was a thrill to see films such as *Gone With the Wind* and *The Sound of Music* at the Strand Theater, a landmark and popular spot in Skowhegan. Seeing a Hollywood film was a special treat, not a regular activity. In summer, we would make it to the Skowhegan Drive-In at least once, squeezing into a car like sardines until we parked, and then we would lay blankets or sleeping bags on the grass and watch the movie under the stars.

To get spending money, we collected returnable beer and soda bottles that people had tossed in the ditch. We hauled them all to Bushey's penny candy store on North Avenue, about a mile or so away, returned them, and bought fistfuls of bubble gum, hot balls, Turkish taffy, Squirrel Nuts, licorice, and root beer barrels—all stuffed into little brown paper bags.

Sam, our black collie-Newfoundland-mix dog, was our regular companion. We dressed him in a black and orange T-shirt and tied ribbons around his tail to attend football games at Skowhegan High School, which was just a few miles across town. He was our team mascot. He wandered all over Skowhegan, and everyone knew him. When the town adopted a leash law, he was delivered to our house in the back seat of a police cruiser more than once before he figured out the drill and fled when he saw cops coming.

We had a Tarzan swing on our property that my brother Matt rigged up by tying a thick rope to the middle of a huge willow tree branch that arched out over a gully. He tied a large knot at the other end of the rope and threw it up to the crotch of the tree. One by one, we'd climb about eight feet up to the crotch, sit on the rope knot, hold on for dear life, and jump out into the gully, swinging back and forth to heights of fifteen to twenty feet until the rope eventually stopped. Motorists sometimes stopped to watch. Some even got out of their cars and tried the swing themselves.

"I'd give three hundred dollars to have that thing in my backyard," one man told us.

My brothers worked on old, inexpensive Chevrolets, Buicks, and Pontiacs in our yard, mostly when our parents weren't home, and drove them around in our large, flat field, over and over, creating a dirt track in the grass. It's a wonder we didn't get killed racing those old wrecks, which we occasionally managed to tip over, sometimes on purpose.

No matter what else we did, our attention would eventually return to the woods. We broke or sawed off fir branches from trees to build lean-tos to play in, chewed spruce gum and checkerberry leaves, lay down on the moss to sip clear water from streams, and climbed birch trees. It was exhilarating to climb a birch tree and then ride the treetop back to the ground and, escaping as fast as we could, watch it snap back up. Climbing a birch is tricky. You must shimmy up a skinny tree trunk—carefully clutching its tiny branches—and wiggle your body toward the tip of the tree until the tree bends and drops you to the ground.

We trekked through the woods and fields to Wesserunsett Stream about a half-mile from our house, crossing neighbors' properties, to dig out the slippery, wet clay from the stream bank, dump it in a bucket, and drag it home to sculpt figures. We rode bikes and horses, shoveled manure for the old man who owned ponies, picked wild raspberries and rhubarb, and ate vegetables, raw, right out of the garden.

Skowhegan in the sixties was a different world, all right. And wouldn't it be nice to go back there, just for a day.

Christmas Memories

It was a special treat to dress up and head out into the dark winter on Christmas Eve to attend the church's midnight candlelight service, long after most people had hunkered down in their warm houses to celebrate.

My family piled into our Ford station wagon and drove downtown, crossed the bridge over the snowy Kennebec River and parked next to the Federated Church, whose colored windows were all lit up for Christmas Eve. Marching inside the warm sanctuary with its high ceilings, red carpet, and red-padded wooden pews, we found comfortable places to sit up front, near the altar, where a large movie screen was set up. When they turned out the lights, the projector started rolling, and we watched the 1938 movie *A Christmas Carol*, based on the classic Charles Dickens tale.

The movie was scary, thrilling, and heartwarming all at the same time. Watching Ebenezer Scrooge as he was visited in the night by ghosts both terrified and fascinated me and was the only part of Christmas I did not totally comprehend. But I loved Reginald Owen's portrayal of Scrooge just the same, and to this day, I watch that movie every Christmas season.

At some point during the evening at church, the choir director handed out Christmas stockings made of red netted material and filled with colorful foil-wrapped candies. Those stockings were precious little gifts. We clung to them as we devoured the story of how Scrooge turned from a sour, stingy man into a loving, generous one.

At midnight, we stood in a large circle in the church, preparing for the candlelight service. We were each given a small candle to hold, encircled with a white paper shield. Standing elbow to elbow, we lit the candles and absorbed the magic as faces gradually emerged from shadow and appeared angelic in the soft light. We sang "Silent Night" and other Christmas carols, mesmerized by the festivities of the evening, and the magic stayed with us as we bundled up to go back out into the cold. We followed the stars home, and even though it was late and we were tired, we fought off bedtime.

Until...

"Listen," my father would say. "I think I hear reindeer on the roof."

We scrambled upstairs and peered through the attic window at the snow on the porch roof, sure that Santa Claus had arrived.

We climbed into bed, but sleep was elusive. We lay, wide-eyed, as Katherine's voice nudged us into dreamland.

"Just close your eyes," my older sister said, "and the next time you open them, it will be Christmas morning."

I remember in 1961, Katherine was right. Dawn did seem to come quickly in the large bedroom over the kitchen that I shared with Jane and Laura, who were one and three years older than me, respectively. We leapt out of bed and hurried down the stairs to the living room where a sea of presents flowed from under the tree.

We were young, but we knew the drill—we could open one gift before everyone else got up. We quickly claimed what we suspected were the gifts we had requested from the Sears, Roebuck & Co. catalog.

Laura tore into hers—a blue ballerina costume, all sparkles and fluff. Jane's outfit was that of a southern belle, a puffy dress flecked with flowers. And I got a nurse's uniform with a cape, cap, and medical bag, complete with faux thermometer and stethoscope.

We donned our new attire and pranced around the house, Laura performing pliés and jetés, Jane, floating like a spirit, and I, cornering them when I could to check temperatures and heart rates.

When we were young, we each got a handful of gifts, for which we were grateful. My mother typically knitted us sweaters and mittens for Christmas, and my grandmothers and our Aunt Barbara always came through with presents.

After we had grown up, we celebrated Christmas Eve at my parents' house, and that tradition continued even after we had all moved away. My father typically roasted a ham; my mother baked fruitcake, stollen bread, and cookies; and everyone brought something to share. By the time our family had grown to include grandchildren and great-grandchildren, the house was full, the gift pile was enormous, and the house shook with laughter and music. My mother played the piano, and we gathered around to sing everything from "Hark! The Herald Angels Sing" to "Rudolph, the Red-Nosed Reindeer."

Now, years later in the quiet of my work space, I can still see and hear the din as clearly as if it were yesterday. It's strange to think my parents are gone, that the house is no longer in the family, and that we all seem to celebrate in our own separate bubbles.

But I like to imagine that, if they listen closely, the people who inhabit our old farmhouse house will hear the ghosts of holidays past, reveling on Christmas Eve.

Finding Our Christmas Tree

We trudged through the woods, my sister and I, looking for just the right Christmas tree. It had stormed the night before, and we were up to our shins in snow, slogging along, scanning the trees, our breath producing white puffs in the frigid air.

"What about this one?" asked Jane, who was carrying the axe. She was pointing to a fir tree with rather skimpy branches.

"No, too thin," I replied. "How about that one?" I said, eyeing a much thicker, plumper one.

"Nope," she said, shaking her head. "That's a cat spruce and will make the house smell like cat you-know-what."

We were teenagers then, old enough to take matters into our own hands when our father declared it was too early to get a Christmas tree. It was about two weeks before Christmas, and Dad always insisted that a week before Christmas was the right time to get a tree, because otherwise it would dry out and become a fire hazard.

For me, waiting that long into the Christmas season to put up a tree was pure torture. Every year, we complained that all our neighbors had their trees up, so why couldn't we?

"Can't we get it this weekend, Dad?" we'd plead. "The Butlers have had theirs up since Thanksgiving!"

But my father wouldn't budge.

As we grew a little older, my brother Matt would trek out into our woods to get the tree. We never knew what he'd come back

18

with. One year, he returned with a tree that was so huge, he had to cut the bottom and the top off once he got it in the house. There it stood in the corner of the living room, a large bush that was beautiful but didn't look much like a tree.

But we didn't care. The tree really was quite lovely after we decorated it with bulbs and tinsel and a star we cut out of cardboard, covered with tinfoil, and hung from the tree's square top. The tree was a testament to the fact that anything can be made beautiful with some effort. In the evenings, we'd sit and gaze at the tree, all lit up with those large and very hot lights; to this day, I don't know why they didn't start a fire and burn the house down.

Those days of struggling to find a good tree and wrangling to make it fit in the corner are over. Now, my husband and I go out and buy one at a roadside stand where there are dozens to choose from, and we always walk away with a tree that's perfect.

Kind of like the one Jane and I finally discovered all those years ago after we traipsed through our parents' woods for what seemed like hours. After searching endlessly for a tree whose height, width, and fullness suited our fancy, we had nearly given up. Tired and cold, we flopped down on the snow and looked wearily skyward. There, we saw what we had been looking for all along—dozens of tall majestic evergreens whose tops were perfectly shaped Christmas trees. It didn't take long for us to decide what we'd do—chop one down and lop off the top.

Taking turns with the axe, we whacked and whaled away at the tree trunk until we made a cut deep enough that we could push the tree over. With a whoosh and the snapping of branches, the tree collapsed in the snow. We chopped off the top eight feet and hauled it home.

No one knew what we had done until springtime when my father went into the woods on Mother's Day to pick flowers for Mom as he did every year. He discovered the swath of downed trees and branches, resembling a war zone, that Jane and I had left behind, and when he got home, we got a lecture about proper forest management.

"But it was a nice Christmas tree, wasn't it, Dad?" we asked.

He just shook his head at our recklessness.

When my husband and I go out to the roadside stand now to choose a tree two weeks before Christmas, it still takes me a long time to find just the right one. If my indecision irritates the man who tends the trees—God bless him—he never shows it.

We bring it home and put it up, and the cats drive us crazy, batting their paws at all the lights and ornaments. And then one evening, as I'm sitting back admiring it and remembering all those trees we had as kids, I'll exclaim out loud, as I do every year, that it's the most beautiful tree in the world.

An Everlasting Gift

It was a snowy night—a blizzard, in fact—and by midnight, the snow had already crept up to the bottom of our dining room windows. It was a Christmas Eve in the sixties, and we were waiting for my mother to get home from work so we could celebrate.

The big evergreen in the living room was glittering with lights and bulbs and tinsel, the gifts were piled high underneath, and holiday treats were laid out on the dining room table, waiting to be consumed. There was smoked sliced ham steaming on an oval platter, salads, mixed nuts, ribbon candy, sugar cookies in the shapes of Christmas trees and angels and decorated with colored frosting, my mother's fruitcake made from scratch, and red punch in a cut-glass bowl with floating frozen raspberries and strawberries.

My mother was an emergency room nurse at Redington-Fairview General Hospital in Skowhegan, and she worked the evening shift, which, in those days, typically meant that she often worked some holidays, and we accepted that fact. When my older siblings became teenagers, we opened our gifts on Christmas Eve instead of in the morning, and if my mother had to work overtime, we knew we just had to wait.

On many nights during the year, she didn't make it home until long after her shift was supposed to end. That's what happens when you work at a small, rural hospital, and there's only a skeleton staff at night. If a car tumbles over a bridge in Solon at ten-thirty, you can't just go home when your shift ends—you must stay until your work is done (which is kind of like a reporter's job, come to think of it).

Anyway, on that Christmas Eve long ago, the snow kept falling and falling. It was a busy night at the hospital. Eleven came and went and then midnight. Although we were all getting sleepy, we waited. It was not Christmas Eve without my mother, who was fun and enthusiastic and loved it when we were all together.

I was the youngest of seven children, so the house was always full of activity year-round—a lot of music and laughter and discussion. On weekends, when we got to stay up late, Mom was delighted if she came home from work and found us still up and sitting around the kitchen table, playing music, making fudge, or doing whatever we did in those days. If we had company, she was doubly pleased.

I always felt fortunate when friends would describe strained relationships with their mothers. I don't believe I ever had a cross word with mine—she was generous, funny, and smart and had more energy than most people half her age.

But as open as she was with most things, she was amazingly private when it came to issues such as her health, and she had her share of health issues during her ninety-two-year life.

When I was little, she had bone cancer and was in the hospital for a year with her leg in traction. We spent Christmas Day in her hospital room. All of us seven children, my father, and my grandmothers filed into Mom's room bearing gifts. I got a large baby doll with a bottle that appeared to drain of its milk as you tipped it to her lips. I was so taken by that phenomenon that when we got home, I broke the bottle apart to see how it worked.

While she was hospitalized, I was scared that Mom might die, but no one talked about that. I lived with a sort of gnawing dread that a seven-year-old couldn't begin to understand, let alone verbalize. But she didn't die, and I remember the day the ambulance brought her home. She was crying, and it was one of the few times I ever saw her cry. I was confused and thought something was wrong. Not until later did I understand she was crying just because she was so happy to be home.

In her later years, after she recovered from cancer, she had a lot of issues with osteoporosis, and her bones broke easily. It seemed she was always undergoing surgeries followed by long, tough recoveries. While we knew she was in pain for much of her life, we never heard her complain.

My mother was a survivor and just kept plugging along, although for many years, she used crutches to get around, even while working at the hospital. She would be embarrassed if she knew I was telling these tales out of school. She didn't focus on her physical ailments and didn't want anyone else to. But when I think back to that Christmas Eve blizzard and the excitement I felt when she arrived home at two in the morning, I think about how resilient she was—and such a positive force.

The local police drove her home in a Jeep, as the roads were barely passable. They couldn't even get into the driveway, which was adrift in snow with more blowing in. The Jeep's headlights illuminated the driveway as the officer escorted her, crutches and all, through the snowdrifts to the house.

She arrived inside, joyful and looking younger than her years, despite having just finished a long and undoubtedly arduous shift at work. She was so happy to be home with us. When I envision the look on her face that early Christmas morning, I am filled with a warmth that really is an everlasting gift.

The Joy of Sledding

On cold winter nights, the neighborhood kids often trekked to the Skowhegan reservoir to skate. We trudged along under the moonlight for about a half-hour, across a large field and through the woods to reach the reservoir, which supplied the town of Skowhegan with drinking water. Once there, we made a beeline for the ice, laid claim to our seats on stumps and fallen trees, removed our boots, and donned our skates.

There was nothing quite as exhilarating as flying across the ice by starlight, scraping away on those old hand-me-down hockey skates, our lungs pumping with cold, fresh air. On those nights, the ice cracked beneath our skates, making a howling noise that both frightened and thrilled us. We knew we wouldn't fall through, because the ice was at least a foot thick.

My brothers, sisters, and I all wore hockey skates. By the time I was a teenager and wore my first pair of figure skates, I thought I'd died and gone to heaven; skating was so much easier in them. I could twirl and fly and skate backwards, seeking to appear much more elegant than I did in those hardscrabble hockey skates. We skated ourselves to exhaustion, dragging ourselves home wet, cold, and bleary-eyed, with barely enough energy to peel off our clothes, find our pajamas, and crawl into bed. By the next morning, we were raring to go again.

When we weren't skating, we were hiking through the snow to a hill near our house, hauling our toboggans and sleds. As usual, we would round up the neighborhood kids and trek eastward to the woods. We pooled our resources and brought whatever goodies we could find to heat over an open fire—cocoa, hot dogs, marshmallows, and Hershey's chocolate. We also used the fire, which my brothers would build, to dry our wet mittens.

Reaching the top of the hill, we piled onto two toboggans, side by side, and shoved off.

"One, two, three—go!"

At the top of the hill, two large pine trees framed the runway. We would aim our sleds to the west and shove off, striking two small

Skating at Morrill Pond in Hartland in 1964. (L to R): Jane Calder, Deborah Miller, Laura Calder, and me. Photo by Donald Miller.

hills of snow before speeding down the long incline, faster and faster until the momentum finally abated and we whimpered to a stop. If it was particularly icy, we could travel faster and farther than usual and, in the end, found ourselves inching up to a barbed-wire fence we all tried to avoid—although more than once, we failed and had the bloody skin to prove it.

Sometimes we raced down the hill with reckless abandon, trying to pull each other off opposing toboggans. Sometimes we set up jumps, catapulting ourselves into the air and landing with a thump on the hard snow. If it was crusty and we fell off the toboggans, our bodies sailed away like giant icicles.

We never tired of being outdoors, whether in the sunshine of summer or darkness of winter. Snow and rainstorms didn't deter us; bad weather merely enhanced the excitement. It was hard work, those childhood adventures, and a lot of fun.

In more recent years, I remember my late father-in-law, lying on the sofa in his nineties, blind from macular degeneration but smiling as he rested. I asked what he was thinking about, and he said his childhood memories. I know that, in my old age, I'll be doing the same, remembering those long-gone winter days in Skowhegan, reveling in the snow.

Valentine's Day
with a Broken Heart

I padded downstairs in my flannel pajamas, making a beeline for the kitchen, where my mother was stirring oatmeal on the stove.

"Mom, I'm feeling a lot better. Can I please go to school today?"

"No," she said. "You have a temp of 101, and you really can't do it."

It was Valentine's Day, and I had the flu. My cheeks were as red and hot as the flames inside the wood stove I sat next to, dangling my feet off the chair and pretending I felt great. If there was one day I didn't want to miss out of the whole school year, it was Valentine's Day.

I attended North Elementary School, which served kids in kindergarten through fourth grade, and I didn't want to miss the party. I knew we'd get those red, white, and pink heart candies with little sayings on them like "Be mine" and "Forever." I also didn't want to miss seeing the looks on my classmates' faces as they opened the Valentines I was planning on giving them. At the time, you could buy Valentine cards at Woolworth's or McLellan's 5-and-10-cent store in downtown Skowhegan. The cards came about thirty to a box and had envelopes to match. You wrote a little note on the back of the card, sealed it, and dropped it in your classmates' Valentine boxes.

The boxes were the best part of the holiday. All the kids brought boxes they had decorated at home for other kids to put their Valentines in.

The teacher lined those lovely boxes up all around the classroom on the windowsills and countertops, right where we could gaze at them all day, admiring the workmanship and imagining what was inside.

Most were fairly typical—a small box covered with tinfoil and red hearts cut out of construction paper. The hearts were stuck on the sides with paste that smelled so good, some kids actually ate it. The box covers, also wrapped with foil, had slits in them for depositing Valentines.

I spent February 13 making my Valentine's box—scrounging up an old shoe box from the attic and covering it with tinfoil, which I tried to make as smooth as a mirror. There was nothing so ugly as a Valentine's box where the tinfoil was all riddled with dents from having been crunched up or put on and taken off the box too many times. Believe me, each year, you could count on seeing some of those. They usually came from kids who crafted their boxes with used tinfoil. Those boxes sat between larger, more elegant ones that contained barely a crease—which you knew someone's mother had helped to make. The thing is, we weren't supposed to get any help with our boxes, because at the end of the party, the teacher chose the best one, and the winner got some kind of prize, like a little bag of candy.

One year, a girl brought in a Valentine's box shaped like a castle, complete with turrets and towers and a moat. It was covered with pretty red paper. We all stared in envy as she placed it proudly on her desk. We knew we didn't stand a chance against it and secretly hoped the teacher would disqualify her, because it was obvious she didn't make it herself. As much as we tried, our psychic pleas to the teacher didn't work. Miss Superiority's castle won, and we knew better than to question the teacher about it. In the end, we didn't really care. We all raced to our boxes, anxious to see what we got for Valentines and who we got them from.

On that Valentine's Day when I was sick, my cards were all written out and in a small pile, ready to take to school. But it was not to be. I begged my mother to let me go, but being a nurse, and a good one, she was unrelenting. Resigned to the fact that I'd experience the Valentine's party in my dreams only, I got up from that kitchen chair and headed to the living room to climb the stairs to bed. That is the last thing I remember before waking up on the floor between the kitchen and dining room, my chin stinging in pain. My mother told me later that when I passed out, I just sort of went straight down, and she heard a loud crack as my chin smacked the floor. I spent Valentine's Day in the emergency room, where the doctor put six stitches in my chin, a sad consolation prize to tout when I returned to school a few days later.

As February 14 rolls around each year, I think of those fancy Valentine's boxes and that unfortunate day I missed the school party. And whenever anyone asks me about the little white line under my chin, I tell them it's my V-Day battle scar.

Salt and Vinegar Fries

While I was passing Bolley's Famous Franks on College Avenue in Waterville the other day, I got to thinking about French fries and the first time I ever tried them with vinegar. It was about fifty-five years ago on a cold, snowy night at Eaton Mountain in Skowhegan.

I was perched at the wooden counter in the snack shack and had just been delivered my paper tray of fries. I was about to indulge when I eyed a vinegar dispenser sitting next to the salt and pepper.

"What's that for?" I asked.

The short-order cook demonstrated how to drench my fries in vinegar after salting them. Although I loved vinegar and olive oil dressing on salad and the mustard pickles from my mother's pantry that were drowned in vinegar, I had never thought of putting it on French fries. It was delicious. After that first taste of vinegar with fries, it became a habit each time I visited Eaton Mountain.

I skied at the mountain many nights during the winters of my childhood, the lights illuminating the trails as I sailed down the slopes again and again. Sometimes it was bitterly cold and windy, other nights milder, but I don't remember ever being deterred by the cold. Skiing was invigorating and exhilarating, and we never tired of it.

The time flew during those evenings, made possible by a recreation program the town hosted. For a minimal fee, we purchased season passes, boarded a school bus outside the municipal building after supper, and traveled the few miles out of town to the mountain.

We wore our heavy ski boots onto the bus, tracking snow and ice into the aisle, and then laid our skis and poles on the back seats in the bus. We plunked ourselves down for the short trip to the mountain, chatting and eager to get out on the slopes.

We skied part way up the mountain via the rope tow, burning holes through our mittens, which prompted us to wear not one but two pairs the next time. That didn't really work either and eventually we discovered that leather was the way to go. I felt sorry for kids just learning to use the rope tow who, grasping the rope for the first time, were catapulted forward, landing flat on their faces in the snow.

The T-bar was more user-friendly, although learning how to use it was, literally, a balancing act, as we were instructed to lean, not sit, on the bar and let it guide us along, up, up, and up the mountain.

The chair lift was the ticket, scooping us up and heaving us to the top of the mountain, although I don't know that I ever fully trusted it. More than once, I imagined the cable snapping and sending us all plummeting to the ground.

Skiing was a regular activity during my school years, but I skied less frequently after I went off to college, only sometimes venturing to Sugarloaf or Saddleback when I returned home for vacation.

Now, my skiing days are long gone, but the memories of those cold nights on the Skowhegan mountain grow more poignant as the years go on and we have a winter where the snow just keeps coming down and down.

Somehow over the years, I managed to let my passion for skiing fall by the wayside, much like my craving for vinegar on fries. But who knows? They say old habits never die, so maybe I'll just revisit both one day.

May Baskets

The month of May always held real promise—promise of warm weather, sunshine, playing outside, and, of course, the impending end of school.

May was also May basket season. During my childhood, many people hung May baskets only on the first day of the month—May Day—but we took the liberty of choosing whatever day we wanted to flock to the candy store, buy reams of sweets, and create a May basket.

May Day is the halfway point between the spring equinox and summer solstice, a time to celebrate the return of spring and coming summer. Traditions vary, but typically in the sixties, schoolchildren would dance around a maypole decorated with ribbons and flowers, and people would surprise their friends and neighbors with May baskets filled with sweets.

As kids, we collected returnable bottles on the side of the road to garner enough cash to buy the candy. To this day, I can conjure up the putrid smell of Schlitz or Narragansett beer, which came in tall brown bottles with long necks and shiny labels. It smelled so abhorrent that I think it's why I never acquired a taste for beer. In any case, there were also Orange Crush bottles to be found, in addition to Coke, root beer, 7UP, and the occasional Moxie bottle.

We'd toss them into a wagon and head to Bushey's candy store on North Avenue in Skowhegan, where we cashed them in to buy hordes of penny candy—mint juleps, red shoestring licorice, root beer barrels, sip-it straws filled with sour powder, Turkish taffy, bubble gum, hot balls, Mary Janes, Squirrel Nuts, Bit-O-Honey, and those tiny wax soda bottles containing sweet colored liquid.

We pointed to what we wanted in the large glass cabinet, and Mr. Bushey, whom I felt an affinity for because his first name was Aimee, would plop our selections into tiny brown paper bags and, with a smile, hand them to us. We traipsed the mile or so back home and, repressing a great urge to consume all the contents along the way, managed to salvage most of the loot and get it home safely.

Then, the fun began of creating the May basket. Typically, we covered a shoebox with colorful crepe paper, taped it on tight, crafted handles for the basket, and tied ribbons on the ends. Then, we filled the basket with candy and waited until dusk.

Deciding who would receive the May basket required a conference earlier in the day of all those involved. We had to reach consensus or at least a majority vote. As the sun neared the horizon, we gathered at a predetermined location and held our final huddle. We would steal our way to the recipient's house and rush, as quietly as possible, to the door, placing the basket on the step and yelling, in unison, at the tops of our lungs, "May basket!"

Then we'd tear away quickly, hiding behind trees and cars, in gullies or in tall grass—anywhere where we could not be found. Aware of the tradition but surprised to be targeted for the honor nonetheless, the kid or kids in the house would come outside and try to find us. It was always a scramble in the dark with leaps, screeches, and laughter, but ultimately, everyone would be found or reveal himself, and we'd all flop on the lawn to share the contents of the basket.

It was a rite of passage as spring changed into summer, these evenings of hanging May baskets on our friends. As we got older, we'd do it to relatives, devising more sophisticated and artistically tasteful baskets bearing gourmet treats. My mother would join us and always got a kick out of it. She had hung May baskets herself as a child, as did her mother before her.

After I graduated from high school and left home, I'd ask new friends if they hung May baskets when they were kids. Inevitably, I'd receive only puzzled looks in return. Most had never heard of the tradition.

Besides feeling sorry for them because of what they'd missed, I was awfully glad to have been raised in rural Maine where such traditions were a part of life.

World Series Offers a Reminder

In the sixties in Skowhegan, the neighborhood kids often gathered to play baseball. The older kids were captains and got to pick teams. It was thrilling to be chosen by Mary, a neighbor who was several years older than me and treated me like I was a valuable player, although assuredly I was merely average. I wasn't much of a hitter, but boy, could I run.

In those days, we had to stomp on the tall grass to make the field suitable for playing, and we used slats of wood for bases. We borrowed our brothers' gloves and bats, which typically were too big for us, but we didn't let that dampen our enthusiasm.

We played until we were exhausted and headed home with dirty limbs, scraped knees, and sometimes minor injuries, as when I got popped in the forehead with a ball.

My three brothers played baseball in school and were good. We were proud to see them play and watch the girls swoon over the players. It was a big deal, being the sibling of a star.

During baseball season, kids talked a lot about players like Carl Yastrzemski and traded baseball cards, both at home and in school. Over the years, our television was always on when the Red Sox played. My father and the boys always watched, but I never was much interested until excitement began to build as World Series time approached. Football never excited me, golf was boring, and I never understood the game of basketball.

But there was something about being in my parents' home in later years, long after I moved away, during the World Series, while my mother—a rabid Red Sox fan—and my father—who also loved the team—were watching. I loved the sounds of cheering and chanting from the crowds audible throughout the house and hearing my mother talking to the players like she was their parent, coaxing, cajoling, cursing, scolding, and praising them.

"C'mon, Pedroia," she'd shout, "You can do better than that."

My father was a good baseball player himself. When he was young, he played semi-pro ball and, in the fourties, was invited to spring training with the St. Louis Cardinals. Unfortunately, he was practicing in Georgia when the telegram was en route to his home in Durham, Maine, and he didn't get it in time. I wonder whether I'd even be here today had he taken a different course in life.

After my father died at ninety-two, my mother continued loving and following the Red Sox, even after she was too frail to climb the stairs and slept in a hospital bed in the dining room, where we placed a large screen TV at the foot of her bed.

It will be four years in January since she died at age ninety-two, but when World Series time rolls around, I can picture her there in that hospital bed, propped up by pillows next to the cat and knitting furiously as she declared her approval or distaste at a particular player's moves.

No matter where you were in the house, you could hear her swearing at a pitcher who didn't perform to her expectations, calling him by name and reprimanding him as if he were right in the room with her.

My interest in baseball isn't anywhere near as acute as was my mother's, so I surprise myself around this time of year when I say I'm not going to watch the World Series but find myself doing so anyway, even though I don't know the players and feel as if I'm an outsider looking in.

I watched the first ten minutes of the Red Sox's first game last month against the Dodgers and went to bed. By the third game, my interest began to pique. I started getting to know players' names (I delighted in saying "Mookie Betts!" aloud) and, like my mother, talked aloud to the television until one in the morning when, tired and bleary-eyed, I hit the sack.

I knew I was addicted when, just before sunrise, I got up and maneuvered my way through a dark house to the living room to check my phone to see who won.

By the final game, I was a crazy fan, hooting and hollering into the night when the Sox scored, despite the fact that we had company asleep in our guest room who surely thought I had gone bananas.

At that point, it all came back: I was a girl running bases around that grassy field in the sixties, the neighborhood kids cheering; I was in my parents' house, the stomping and chanting from Fenway Park blaring out over the TV airwaves and my folks exclaiming their praise or disapproval.

For a few precious days last month during the World Series, we had a reprieve from the nastiness and violence that has pervaded our lives. We got to remember it wasn't so long ago that we were in a saner world, enjoying a tradition our country loves and cherishes. We were happy, hopeful, fun-loving—and united. (Nov. 5, 2018)

Summertime at the Swimmin' Hole

Over many years since childhood, in the various places I visited or lived, I always sought out the best places to swim.

During the hot steamy summer days of the sixties, it was White Bridge. White Bridge was the swimming hole in Skowhegan that we frequented as kids. I don't think the bridge was really white—it was so marred with dirt and dust from traffic on West Ridge Road that it was hard to tell—but that's what we called it.

"Dad, can we go to White Bridge?"

It was only about a mile away, the bridge that spanned a branch of Wesserunsett Stream, and we'd pile into the station wagon, crowding in there like wiggling piglets, hot, sticky, and ready to hit the cold water. We parked beside the road and were out the doors before the car came to a full stop.

It was a steep incline over a grassy embankment to the stream, and we raced down and took flying leaps into the water beneath the bridge overhead. The water was brown and murky, but we didn't care. As long as we managed to stay away from the opposite bank of the narrow stream where the dreaded bloodsuckers lurked, we were golden. I remember some neighborhood kids straying from the safe zone, emerging from the muddy water with bloodsuckers all over their ankles, their mothers hauling out the salt to rub all over them until they fell off. I was never so unfortunate as to suffer the ravages of a bloodsucker and was glad of it.

When we were a little older, Lake George in Canaan was the swimming hole of choice. My friend Patty's father drove his pickup down our road, stopping at every house inhabited by kids. We'd climb into the back and hang on tight. The six-mile trip to Canaan was bumpy and wild.

We giggled and gabbed, hair flying, towels wrapped around our torsos, bugs splattering in our eyes and getting caught in our throats. The old truck rocked and lurched, and we squealed in unison. It was all part of the excitement. We turned north toward the lake, rumbled up the dirt road, and piled out of the truck, tossing towels onto the rocks and diving into the cool, pristine water, which, to this day, remains clear and unpolluted.

Ah, the long days of summer.

On the Fourth of July, we swam in the ocean at Pemaquid Beach, emerging blue and quivering from the frigid water. We loved the salt and sun, buried our bodies in the sand, and ran again into the waves.

When I was thirteen, we found a particularly special swimming hole at Walton's Bridge in Cornville. We drove east down a dirt road off the West Ridge until it turned grassy, left the car there, and descended a steep incline onto large rocks that arched down into the water. We'd dive into the deep, cold pool over and over again and then lie, exhausted, on the rocks, gazing up at the old bridge that once connected the west to the east ridge but had long since been out of use.

I got my first camera at Walton's Bridge—a Kodak Instamatic. I found it on the rocks one rainy day. It was a small, metal rectangular camera that took great pictures and became my prized possession, launching me into a lifelong love of photography.

It's interesting that so many people are drawn to water, wherever we go. Beyond my childhood and beyond Maine, I've swum in the lakes and rivers in Massachusetts and Connecticut, the ocean in Oregon, Florida's Gulf Coast, the Caribbean, even the gorgeous blue Mediterranean Sea off the Isle of Capri in southern Italy.

They were all lovely, but none compare to the old swimming holes of my childhood, which drew us in and called us back every summer. They belonged to us. We didn't have to ask for permission to go there or pay admission. Waking up in the heat of summer and anticipating a trek to the swimming hole was exhilarating. I can't think of much else that lent such pure joy.

Penny for Your Thoughts

The other day, we were driving across Memorial Bridge over the Kennebec River in Augusta when Phil remembered paying a ten-cent toll to cross it in the fifties and sixties.

I pondered that for a minute.

"It took a lot of dimes to amount to much," I said. "A thousand cars to garner a mere one hundred dollars."

Of course, a dime was worth a lot more in those days.

When I was growing up in Skowhegan, the ice cream man came around in a pudgy white truck, a bell ringing and a tune playing as it approached. It cost five cents for a Popsicle or a Fudgesicle, but if you had a dime, you could buy a more deluxe treat—an ice cream sandwich. My older sister Katherine always had the extra cash and could afford the latter while we younger kids got the cheap treats.

I was fascinated by the white puffs of air that wafted out of the small door on the side of the truck when the ice cream man opened it to retrieve our purchases. He also sold Pine Cone ice cream on a stick, which consisted of vanilla ice cream in the shape of a pine cone, dipped in chocolate. If, after consuming it, you found a red tip on the end of the stick, you got a free one.

We also bought candy for next to nothing when we were kids. One cent would net you a piece of bubble gum or two pieces of certain kinds of candy, such as root beer barrels or those striped straws that had sour sugar inside. With a nickel, you could get a slab of Turkish taffy or a peanut butter cup.

When we were really little, my grandmother would give us each a dollar to buy Christmas presents. You'd be surprised at what a dollar would buy. I got presents for the whole family at McLellan's store in downtown Skowhegan. Pencils, pens, paper, candy—all were a nickel each. I thought I'd died and gone to heaven.

What does a dime or a dollar get you now?

In 1958, my parents bought our rural, five-bedroom house on a nice, flat lot with thirty acres, part field, part woods, for $7,000. We had a big barn, a shed connecting it to the house, a long chicken coop, and a garage. It was heaven growing up there.

When I went off to college in Connecticut in the seventies, everyone told me I was crazy because tuition, room, and board cost $5,000 a year. You could attend University of Maine for a fraction of that—still a lot of money in those days—but a more reasonable choice, they said. I was fortunate to be able to pay off my school loans by the time I was thirty. Now, when I hear younger colleagues talk about their enormous college debt, I feel both really sorry and scared for them.

Inflation is something, isn't it?

I'm trying to remember the last time I paid a dime for anything. I guess it was about twenty years ago for a cup of really bad coffee from a machine in the lunchroom, which was off a hallway in the newsroom. You stuck a dime in the slot, a tiny paper cup dropped down, and this lukewarm, grayish liquid drizzled into it.

It was pretty terrible, but at midnight when you were struggling to pound out a story from a council meeting that went on way too long, it was better than nothing.

Kind of like the little pile of groceries you can buy now for a hundred bucks: better than nothing.

Fourth of July by the Ocean

I can't inhale the scent of a wild rose without thinking of my maternal grandmother, Nettie Rowell, who grew a healthy crop of bushes by her porch in Cornville when I was growing up.

It was her summer house, and to this day, I believe I love the smell of roses and fresh-cut grass because visiting her proved to be some of the happiest times in my life. For years, whenever our family spent the Fourth of July at Pemaquid, the wild pink roses that lined the paths to the beach threw off a scent so poignant that it engendered visions of my grandmother, who would make sachets of rosebuds and place them in bureau drawers. She has been gone more than half a century now; although when July Fourth rolls around, I think of her.

She was a schoolteacher and lived with us in Skowhegan at times when we were children. She gently corrected us when we'd command "Lay down, Sam" to our big black Newfoundland-collie mix. "It's lie down, Sam—lie down," she'd say. She taught us to sew and cook and recite poetry out loud during long summer evenings.

My grandmother, whom we addressed as "Marnie," was a disciplinarian but a gentle one. She issued the three of us youngest girls specific chores and required that we complete them before going out to play. She directed us to create chore boards on which we glued pictures we had cut out of magazines of the various rooms of the house we were to clean: Laura was to polish the furniture and vacuum the dining room, Jane to clean the living room, and I, the hall stairs and bathroom. We perused magazines to find pictures of said rooms, clipped them out, glued the pictures to the board, and wrote our names in large letters next to them. When we got tired of cleaning the same rooms, we were allowed to swap. My grandmother took care of the kitchen, and of course, we were responsible for our own bedrooms.

A trip to the ocean on the Fourth of July with her and the rest of our family was a big deal. We went to bed early, but we were too excited to sleep. Late that night, my mother would fry chicken in the electric skillet and bake chocolate-bit cookies, brownies, and divinity fudge. Early on the Fourth, she made cream cheese and olive sandwiches and lemonade, packed the picnic basket, and corralled us into the old Ford station wagon.

Wearing bathing suits under our shorts and schlepping towels, we piled into the car for the eighty-mile trip to Pemaquid, in the town of Bristol.

On what seemed like an endless drive to Pemaquid Beach, we asked, repeatedly, "Are we there yet?"

We'd arrive at the beach, choose a spot on the white sand near the roses, and charge to the water. It was a daylong adventure in the salt air, riding the cold waves, traipsing along the beach, and collecting shells.

Later, we'd visit the lighthouse at Pemaquid Point, where we climbed on the giant rocks to watch the waves rush in. When we were older, we perused the nearby gift shop and then drove to New Harbor for a lobster dinner on the wharf. On the drive home, we stopped at the general store in Round Pond for shopping and ice cream.

We still make summer forays to the lighthouse and wharf, although not on the holiday, and haven't visited the beach in several years.

Things change, and this July Fourth will be quiet, particularly as we maneuver our way through a pandemic that has forced us to adapt to challenges and alter our traditions, especially those involving the gathering of friends and family. But we've got happy memories of those past holidays to sustain us.

And I'm fairly sure that, armed with our innate Maine ingenuity, we'll find ways to have a fun and safe holiday weekend.

The Skowhegan State Fair

I stood peering over the top of Grammie's buffet in our dining room, checking the level of coins in my glass jar.

I was a kid in the sixties, saving up money for the Skowhegan State Fair, which arrived in late summer every year. Collecting enough quarters, nickels, and dimes to fill the jar to its screw-on cover took a long time. I saved all year, watching the collection grow. As I did, I dreamed of cotton candy, candied apples, Ferris wheel rides, and bizarre characters who annually inhabited the fairgrounds.

There were sword swallowers, giant snakes, fire eaters, and scantily clad women dancing on stages with drawn curtains, trying to lure men into their girly shows. There were creatures billed as half-human or half-animal, bearded ladies, and houses of horror.

Weeks before the fair arrived, my brain went wild, imagining all those strange and interesting people, including folks who came into town from the willywacks once a year and whom I loved to watch.

We kids were bug-eyed at the odd toys and stuffed animals hanging from game booths where you could fire a pop gun, toss rice bags, or throw darts to score a prize. One year, I took home a cheap tiny plastic doll tied to the end of a stick for successfully hitting a target with a fake handgun. I eyed my prize curiously for days afterward.

It was August, and the fair represented the last hurrah for us kids before we headed back to school after Labor Day. The mornings were cool, the afternoons hot and dry, and the aromas wafting from the fairgrounds enticing.

Onions and hot dogs sizzled on open stovetops, French fries cooked in giant vats of hot oil, and cotton candy spun around on sticks behind glass windows. It all sent us swooning and salivating.

Eerie tunes blasted from the merry-go-round, whose horses seemed to be alive, their eyes following us as they whizzed up, down, and around. Signs along the midway advertised beano games, beds of nails, frogmen, and fortune tellers.

For an admission fee, you could patronize sideshows to view the so-called "freaks of nature." I was drawn to those oddities every year, including the one boasting the only surviving man with no head, no arms and no legs—"You'll NEVER see this again in your LIFETIME!" a recorded voice screamed to passers-by.

I was hooked. I paid my dollar and entered a dark tent with other curiosity seekers, marching in single file along a roped-in, grassy corridor and stopping to peer into a wooden box illuminated from above by a lightbulb. My hopes plummeted as we found ourselves gaping at what clearly was a man's torso crafted from a brown paper bag painted the color of flesh with an electronic mechanism underneath causing it to beat like a heart.

A few more admissions to shows like that over the years cured me of my yearnings, affording me more cash to spend on rides and treats.

The fair, the oldest continuously running agricultural fair in the country, also offered the mundane in the 4-H and Grange exhibits, packed with shelves of baked goods and fresh garden produce that, toward the end of the fair, had turned wilted and moldy.

Women sold fudge, sweaters, and hand-sewn dolls in the exhibit halls while outside, farmers sheared sheep and milked cows in the agricultural barns. Under the ice arena, spectators lined the bleachers to watch tractor pulls and equestrian competitions. The grandstand also packed in fairgoers who came to see country music stars and big bands or watch harness racing.

My favorite part of the fair, though, cost nothing and left me with the best memories of all. I had the privilege of accompanying my father, a horse lover, to the fairgrounds early mornings when all was quiet and the dew was still on the grass.

We visited the racehorses, stabled in long, low barns at the northern edge of the fairgrounds. They munched on hay, nudged their stall mates—often a dog or cat—and poked their heads over the stall doors to check us out. We brought carrots and apples to feed them and enjoyed feeling their warm muzzles on our palms as they snatched and chewed them up.

During fair week, I'm always transported back to those lazy mornings when the scent of hay wafted through the stables and the only sounds were our voices and the tap, tap, tap of a farrier shoeing a horse in a nearby stall.

My Camelot

About a week before I went to see *Camelot* at the Waterville Opera House, I started whistling and singing songs from the show. Back in the seventies, when I worked summers at Lakewood Theatre in Madison, I watched *Camelot* a lot, so I already knew the songs.

Memories of Lakewood came flooding back after the show when I dropped by the orchestra pit and ran into Becky Eldridge, a flutist who also played for the Lakewood production of *Camelot* so long ago.

"That was thirty years ago," she said.

She looked a little older, but not much. We marveled at the time that had passed from one *Camelot* to the next.

"Where did thirty years go?" I asked.

The site on Lake Wesserunsett, which was to become Lakewood Theatre, was a swampy amusement park at the turn of the twentieth century. The first stage play performed there was *The Private Secretary* and opened on June 15, 1901, which is considered the birthday of the modern Lakewood Theatre. The oldest continuously running summer theater in the United States, Lakewood is known as the State Theatre of Maine.

For me, in the seventies, it was like *Camelot*, where every day seemed new and exciting. Actors would come and stay at the lake for a week—that's how long each show ran—and we got to know them both onstage and off.

At Lakewood, it was always sunny, with a continuous warm wind blowing off the lake onto the grassy lawn where we played bocci, sunned ourselves in white Adirondack chairs, and generally lolled about on our off-time.

I was a box office assistant for two summers and box office manager for a third. The staff worked hard all day and socialized in the evenings at the Inn. It was loud with laughter, color, and fun, and we hobnobbed with people like Milton Berle, Lana Turner, Imogene Coca, Maureen O'Sullivan, John Raitt, and Sylvia Sidney, all of whom are gone now.

Farley Granger, who played Dracula one summer, invited me to dine with him one evening at the Lakewood Inn by the theater, and we had a marvelous time, chatting and laughing like two old chums. Being in my twenties at the time, I hardly knew who he was, which I think endeared me to him.

One week during the summer of 1978, *Arsenic and Old Lace* was featured, and two lovely older actors, Louise Kirtland and Anita Webb of New York City, played the leads.

I had just finished my shift in the box office one chilly night, and we box office employees joined the actors at the Lakewood Inn after the show, as we did most nights, to socialize, tell stories, and get to know each other. It was a magical time, those theater days, when patrons dressed in their finery traveled from far and wide to see the shows, and the atmosphere was filled with music, dance, and drama.

We entered the warm inn and sat around low tables in comfy chairs, soaking in the excitement of the evening. That night, Kirtland and Webb were my tablemates, and we chatted about everything under the sun. I, being a thin, young, twenty-something at the time, was cold and shivering from the damp night air, and the glamorous Kirtland noticed that my teeth were chattering.

"You need a Brandy Alexander to warm you up, my dear!" she exclaimed.

I knew little about alcoholic drinks, and they all sounded and looked very sophisticated. Kirtland ordered me a Brandy Alexander, and it came in a pretty goblet, all chocolaty-looking and topped with a sprinkling of nutmeg. One sip, and I was dazzled. Although the brandy was sharp, it warmed my throat and took away the chill.

I never forgot the name of that drink and the way it rolled effortlessly off my tongue when I told stories of Lakewood years later, including those about my friendship with Kirtland and Webb, two fine actresses who liked me so much that they invited me to visit them in New York City after they left Lakewood. I took them up on that offer the following April.

It was an easy trip to the city, since I was attending college in Connecticut and could take the train. I stayed at the Taft Hotel and attended a Broadway show with Kirtland and Webb, and we shared a delightful dinner at Sardi's restaurant. It was a fun evening, made even more interesting when the actor and comedian Charles Nelson Reilly stopped by our table and, after being introduced to me, kissed my hand. He was a bit in his cups that evening. He and the women bantered and chortled and reminisced, and I just soaked in every minute.

During my summers at Lakewood, I also struck up a friendship with the actor Kevin Tighe from the television show *Emergency!*, although I knew nothing of the show when I met him. We shared a love of literature, and he introduced me to the works of Flannery O'Connor, whose writings I grew to love. Although he lived in California, he visited New York occasionally. I traipsed around the city with him one weekend, and we had a grand time eating, visiting music stores, and watching movies.

Me and some of my siblings in 1970. (L to R): Me, Katherine, Matthew, Laura, and Jane.

On another evening at Lakewood, Milton Berle joined a handful of the staff for a lobster dinner in one of the Lakewood cottages. We stayed up until about four in the morning, Berle telling us stories about vaudeville and keeping us entertained. He was very social and most generous with his time, and I think he loved Lakewood and us.

John Raitt, father to blues singer Bonnie Raitt, was also a lot of fun, as were Lynn Redgrave, Imogene Coca, Sylvia Sidney, Della Reese, and Maureen O'Sullivan, Mia Farrow's mother. And Lana Turner was just plain elegant.

The theater staff liked to order meals from Momma Baldacci's restaurant, which was on the road to Skowhegan and where the food was exemplary and the family large, gracious, and friendly. A young John Baldacci—yes, the man who would go on to be Maine's governor—worked at the Baldacci's in Bangor and called the Lakewood box office nearly every day to make theater reservations for restaurant patrons who would dine at the Madison Baldacci's and then come to Lakewood to see a show. I can still hear that distinct and concisely cheerful voice on the telephone: "Hi Amy, John Baldacci. I need four seats in orchestra right, as close to the aisle as possible." We girls in the box office spent the whole summer talking with him by phone about tickets before finally meeting him one night when he came for a show.

Life at the theater was a world unto its own—a carefree, magical, dreamy place where the lines between fantasy and reality blurred— and we loved every minute of it. Our heads were filled with music and fairy tales. We recited lines from plays and sang the songs from musicals such as *Camelot, Carnival,* and *My Fair Lady* as we strolled about the grounds, absorbed in the magic.

If I try very hard, I can imagine myself back in that mystical place of happy endings, where life was young and our futures stretched before us with unlimited possibility.

Kind of like Camelot.

Education on the School Bus

These cool, crisp mornings, as school buses rumble along the roads, I feel a twinge of nostalgia for all the years I rode the bus to and from school in Skowhegan.

For me, the bus was as much a part of my life as school itself. In fact, I still dream about being perched in those old green seats, lurching to and fro as we bounced across bridges, sailed past farmhouses and hayfields, and ground through the downtown, windows open in spring and fall, the smell of diesel wafting in. In winter, with windows frozen shut, we pressed noses against the glass, peering out, rubbing away the window fog with wet mittens.

The bus was a place we could engage in conversation or turn away and watch the world go by. It also was a gold mine for curious kids like me who loved to watch people and listen to them talk.

The first day of school meant getting to inspect everyone's new attire—the sophisticated high school girls with their mini-skirts, white go-go boots, red lipstick, and hair wrapped up in beehives; boys in pressed shirts and trousers; we younger girls in jumpers, ankle socks, and patent leather shoes. We sported new pencil cases—those rectangular pouches that came in various colors and zipped shut—filled with newly sharpened colored pencils, erasers, and yellow No. 2s. We also lugged spiral notebooks and, of course, brown paper bags containing our cold lunches.

There were the poor kids, whose rumpled clothes were hand-me-downs or those left over from last year, and I felt sorry for them. Their shoes were worn and scuffed, and I don't know if they ever got to eat lunch, now that I think of it.

The older girls talked about boys; the boys talked about girls.

I remember our bus passing the home of a high school science teacher whose pretty wife was outside in a chaise lounge, sunbathing in a two-piece suit. One boy said that's why the teacher always came to school looking tired, prompting laughter from his friends. I was too young to understand what they meant but figured it out much later.

The bus was where we gossiped, got the scoop, laid plans, and learned about life. One day, my friend Dawn, who grew up on a farm, informed me about the facts of life as we sat in the second row behind the bus driver. I thought her theory strange and didn't believe it.

On the school bus on November 22, 1963, we first learned about tragedy. President John F. Kennedy had been assassinated in Dallas, and schools closed early. We kids were sent home on the bus, though I did not really grasp the meaning of what was happening until we picked up the older kids at the high school, and they were all discussing it. I remember exactly where we were when the reality of it hit me: in the high school parking lot heading toward Main Street. Some of the kids were crying.

Also on the bus, I had my last conversation with a longtime childhood friend, Dicky Marshall, who drowned in the Kennebec River shortly thereafter. Dicky lived a few houses around the corner from us and took part in our daily adventures, from fishing in the Wesserunsett Stream that ran through the woods behind his house to building snow forts and tunnels, tree houses, and cabins in the woods. One summer, we constructed several enormous teepees from piles of boards a logging company had discarded and left in a nearby field. Our project was so unusual, the local newspaper came and took a photo of us sitting near the teepees, cross-legged and looking very proud.

Right before Dicky was swallowed up by the river one Saturday morning in spring, we had a lively discussion on the bus about all the crazy fun we had as little kids. We were in seventh grade and sitting in the back of the bus, he in one seat and I in the next, talking a mile a minute, telling stories. Dicky and I had the love of stories and laughter in common, and the more we pontificated, the more animated and loud we got. I remember his cheeks were as red as the army jacket he loved to wear, his dark brown hair framing a joyful face I shall never forget.

It was the last time I saw Dicky and a memory I hold dear a half-century after his death.

We never thought much about the bus drivers all those years and took for granted they would always be there. Some were characters and talked a lot while others barely said a word, but they knew all of us by name and exactly where we lived and were never late in picking us up.

I heard on the news the other day that school bus drivers are in such great demand across the country that they're recruiting military veterans to do the work. Times change, and so do we.

But what will not fade are memories of riding that bus—and they become particularly vivid around Labor Day, which, in our youth, marked the last day of summer freedom. Even that has changed, as kids now return to school a week earlier—and some adults think they should go year-round.

What? No summer vacation? I can't imagine it. But that's a topic for another day.

I Love Apples

"Hi Marnie!"

I slammed the kitchen door, dropped my books on the bench, and called out to my maternal grandmother, who was waiting for us when we arrived home from school. Marnie was a retired schoolteacher who owned a summer house in Cornville, but in the winter, she alternated staying with her half-sisters, who also lived in Skowhegan, our aunt Barbara in Windsor, or us at our house. When she was staying with us and we arrived home from school, there were always fresh-baked cookies on the table, as we typically were famished when we got off the bus. If we wanted something more to eat, Marnie directed us to the bushels of apples that we kept in a room off the kitchen we referred to as the "back room," an area that later would disappear when we tore the wall down between the two rooms to expand the kitchen.

I can see them now: Northern Spy, Cortlands, McIntosh and—if we were lucky—Red Delicious.

In a deep closet off our dining room, my mother kept the jars of jam and jelly she made, as well as produce from the garden, including tiny pickled beets, mustard pickles, and peaches. When I was young, my older sister Katherine and I would sometimes get a hankering for pickled beets late at night and raid the pantry. Those beets were delicious.

Mom also made crab apple jelly, using small crab apples she plucked from a tree in the backyard of my grandmother's Cornville house—a tree my mother continued to collect apples from long after my grandmother had died and the house was sold. As my mother aged, the new owners were kind enough to deliver crab apples to my mother in the fall.

To make the jelly, which also was stored in her pantry, she boiled the apples in a large pot and spooned them into a cheesecloth bag she hung from a cupboard door handle. It was fascinating to watch the red liquid drip, drip, drip into a bowl she placed beneath it.

Apples in general were a staple of autumn, and we devoured them as if they were candy. When October rolled around, the house was often filled with the aroma of that sweet fruit baking in various forms—apple pie, apple crisp, or just plain old baked apples in a casserole dish, dripping with juice, the skins still on. We sometimes had applesauce or applesauce cake.

Maine apples, I think, are the best around. In the sixties, apples were a special fall treat. We climbed many an apple tree to pluck the fruit off branches, not thinking twice about a wormhole here and there; we just munched around them.

Early in the fall, our impatience got the better of us and we ate green apples by the bushel, no matter that they were sour and might give us stomachaches. There was nothing like biting into a green apple and then shaking a good dose of salt on the white pulp before taking another.

And, of course, there was apple cider. I remember a man named Charlie who sold us bushels of apples and bottles of cider. He was always outdoors, and his cheeks were red and round and shiny, just like apples. As a little girl, I imagined that he ate so many apples that he came to look like one.

As we grew older, we visited apple orchards in October. Now, they're these fancy places where you can take a hayride, pick your own apples, and buy apple products like pies, cider, doughnuts and apple butter. It's a chance for those of us who used to spend our entire existence outdoors, but who are now relegated to a life of work and responsibility, to step back in time.

There's nothing so sweet as taking a walk in the cold October air, dry leaves swishing underfoot, the skyline awash in red and yellow. There's no place like Maine in the fall, that short-lived, magical time between summer and winter, when reaping the harvest is reward for our summer work. And if plentiful, it gives us a winter of local bounty.

Mom and Apple Pie

Try as I might, I'll never be able to replicate my mother's and maternal grandmother's apple pies. I have the recipes all right, but there was something about theirs that puts mine to shame.

They would toss the flour into a bowl, add a few splashes of ice water and bits of cold butter, fork it all up, and cut the dough in two pieces for the upper and lower crusts. In what seemed like seconds, they had deftly rolled them out, folded the crusts in half, and readied them for the pie plate. To this day, I'm impatient when it comes to peeling and coring apples, but they were able to do it swiftly, seamlessly, while chatting with us kids or even talking on the phone. The kitchen smelled like heaven while their pies baked in the oven.

As little girls, my sisters and I learned how to make pies from both my mother and grandmother, and the tricky part, we found out quickly, was the crust. Too much water and the dough was too sticky to work with; not enough, and it was dry and made the baked crust like cardboard.

I always liked to sample the raw dough; it was salty-sweet and yummy. I loved the way my mother used the leftover dough after she trimmed around the top crust. She'd gather all the dough scraps, mold them into a ball, roll it out flat like a crêpe, and brush melted butter all over it. Then she'd sprinkle it with a generous amount of sugar and cinnamon mixed together. She rolled the dough into a log, flattened it somewhat, and cut it into pieces, placing them onto a cookie sheet for baking.

What a sensory experience it was, peering through the oven's glass window to watch the butter and cinnamon bubbling at the edges of the dough, which grew as it baked. The aroma was intoxicating. There was nothing like sinking our teeth into one of those warm, buttery pastries for which we would praise my mother, who saw the operation as merely a practical way to make use of leftover dough. When they came out of the oven, they were sweet slices of pure joy—hot, sugary, and succulent.

The Old Tricks and Treats

Halloween was a big holiday for us kids—almost as important as Thanksgiving and Christmas. Kids nowadays probably won't understand this, because candy is everywhere and readily available in big stores—shelves and shelves of it, packaged in large plastic bags for Halloween. But when I was growing up, it wasn't as plentiful nor were there so many varieties.

A few days before Halloween, mothers went to the store and bought a package of tiny white paper bags that had black and orange Halloween designs on the front, typically of a witch on a broomstick flying off into the sky.

They packed those bags with popcorn or several pieces of candy, like Tootsie Rolls, Squirrel Nuts, mint juleps, and bubble gum. Then they folded up or stapled the end of the bag, plopped it into a large bowl with the others, and handed them out to the goblins and ghouls who came to the door chanting "Trick or treat!"

When I was small, my mother made candied apples, spearing them with little wooden sticks and dipping them into sticky red caramel. Sometimes she'd roll them in a bowl of chopped peanuts before placing them on a sheet of waxed paper to harden.

Her candied apples were delicious—even better than the ones we got at the Skowhegan State Fair in late summer. Once the apples hardened, my mother carefully wrapped them in waxed paper and handed them out. Many kids knocked at the door every year just for those candied apples.

Halloween costumes were typically created based on whatever we could find around the house, and with a little ingenuity, the garb could be pretty creative. A scarecrow came to life using an oversized plaid flannel shirt, dungarees shredded at the knee, and hay stuffed up the sleeves; a witch materialized from an old black dress, a hat made of cardboard painted black, lots of red lipstick, and charcoal to outline the eyes.

My mother often worked late into the night assembling costumes for us on her old Singer sewing machine. She could whip up the most incredible attire on that contraption. When we were very little, we just wore plastic face masks, the store-bought kind that got all sweaty and wet after you wore them a while. It felt great to shed them in the cold night air while trekking between houses.

We traveled in groups, feeling safe in our disguises as we faced strangers at their doorsteps. Some were friendly and generous; others peered at us from inside their darkened houses, never opening the door. We imagined they hated little kids and would as soon cook us for supper as toss us a treat. The imagined danger gave us an eerie thrill, as did our tendency to wander farther from home than we were allowed.

In Skowhegan, older kids carried pillow cases instead of paper bags—claiming you could carry a lot more candy that way. Some even ventured across the Kennebec River where only the most courageous dared go. It wasn't that the south side of the river was scary for any reason; it's just that if you went there trick or treating, some homeowners would ask where you lived, and if you said you were from across the river, they sent you packing.

When we finally headed home—cold, tired, and bedraggled—we dumped our loot onto the living room floor, comparing the size of our hauls. If I close my eyes, I am transported back to those Halloweens of my childhood. I can still feel the cold October night, sense the mask against my face, and smell the sweet aroma of my mother's candied apples.

Black Casket, Three Miles Away!

"Black casket, three miles away, coming to get you!"

I still get the heebie-jeebies when I hear my sister's voice in my head tell me that ghost story. Laura used to love telling me scary stories when I was little, particularly around Halloween when the

55

skies were dark, leaves blew around the house at night, and you could hear the wind whirring outside.

Laura, three years older than me, knew a lot of stories, some of which she made up as she went along, but it was her tale about the black casket that really got to me.

That darned casket would get closer and closer until it was only two miles away and then only one mile and then finally she'd screech "Black casket, I'm in the kitchen, I'm in the living room, I'm in your bedroom. I've GOT YOU!"

I'd scream and dive under the covers and not come out until morning. Oh, how I hated those scary stories, and oh, how I loved them at the same time.

"Tell us a ghost story," I'd plead.

Laura would always come up with something. Like the one about the man with the golden arm.

"Give me my gooooolden arm!" she'd say, stretching the word out and making her eyes pop out of her head. I don't remember the particulars about that story, but it was spooky.

She claimed some of her stories were about real people, like the man with the white beard and checkered shirt. She said she would wake up in the middle of the night, and he was in her room, scrounging around in her belongings. She referred to him as "The Man," so that's what I and my sister, Jane, called him, too.

I think Laura read too many Nancy Drew mysteries, because she was always playing detective and trying to devise plans to catch The Man. One time, she raided my mother's cupboard and brought a bag of Gold Medal flour upstairs to sprinkle all over the floor of our bedroom. She swore he was real and would prove it by capturing his footprints.

When none appeared the next morning, she piled books against the bedroom door and said when he entered the next night, the books would crash onto the floor and wake us all up, and we'd pounce on him and call the police.

That did not produce results either, so Laura got this big idea in her head. She'd get our neighborhood friend Carla Perkins to dress up in Laura's blue ballet tutu and try to lure The Man into a trap by acting seductive. Carla looked pretty ridiculous dancing around in that tutu, her skinny ten-year-old legs all scratched up from playing in the woods the day before. I didn't figure any intruder would be attracted to her in that condition. I guess I was right, because we never did catch The Man. Despite Laura's directive that we stay awake into the wee hours of the night to nab him, we all crashed sometime after midnight. I decided if The Man was real, the sight of Carla scared him off.

After school, we'd watch the television show *Dark Shadows* about a vampire named Barnabas Collins, despite an order from my grandmother not to watch it. I also snuck downstairs late one Saturday night to watch a show called *Weird* that my older siblings watched and was about werewolves and other awful creatures. I had nightmares after that, so I never watched it again.

A Youth on Horseback

I perused the flea market in the old North Vassalboro mill, eyeing the horse-related items for sale.

There were saddles—both Western and English—bridles, bits, blankets, earrings in the shapes of horses, jewelry boxes with horses painted on them, and even bracelets made of horsehair. This all served to strike a longing deep inside for my carefree childhood days riding horses—sometimes English, most times Western, and, when I was particularly brave, bareback.

There were several horses in our Skowhegan neighborhood, and when I was thirteen, I wintered a horse from a stable and kept it from September through June. He was a large horse, beautiful and sleek, chestnut-colored with a white stripe down his face.

I called him Heisan on the advice of my sister's boyfriend, who insisted he deserved a name that sounded regal. I convinced my father to build a horse stall inside the barn, complete with a door that opened both on the top and bottom like the one in the TV show about the talking horse Mr. Ed.

That year, I contracted migratory arthritis, and all my joints ached. The doctor thought having a horse and riding would help heal my condition and ease the pain. I wore special brown leather shoes that laced up and weren't very fashionable but soothed my aching arches.

Those shoes always seemed to smell like horse manure, but I didn't care. I wore them every day as I fed and watered Heisan, removing them only to change into boots for cleaning the stall and spreading fresh straw. Every day in the fall and spring—and when feasible in winter—I saddled up and took off riding through the fields and woods, up the Malbons Mills Road to my friend Pandy's house or to Linda's or Peggy's. They all had horses, and I rode with whoever was game on any particular day. The more I rode, the more I forgot about my pain.

I rode through the cool, crisp days of autumn, Heisan ambling through the dry, crackling leaves. I'd take him out in the winter snow if it wasn't too deep, and he'd prance around the field, blowing steam from his nostrils and kicking snow up into the air.

One spring day, as I was riding in an abandoned cow pasture, Heisan got spooked and took off full bore, bucking me out of the saddle and sending me airborne, landing me on his neck. I held on for dear life as he bolted into the woods, branches and trees snapping back and striking me all over until he finally calmed down and headed home with me looking like I had been dragged through a rose bush.

By the time summer approached, my arthritis had subsided, and I bounced out of bed each day, anxious to get to the barn and saddle up. Those were happy mornings. Heisan would hear me coming and stomp around in the stall, poke his head out the top of the door, and greet me, his intense brown eyes watching my every move. He was as anxious as I was to hit the road. We'd gallop into the field, canter down the woods road among the evergreens, find a stream where Heisan would take a cool drink, and sit for a while, listening to the water run.

Now, decades later, the horse stall is closed up and used for storage, the shelves and hooks outside it that once held brushes, bag balm, and bridles empty. There's no longer the scent of hay wafting through the barn when the front and back doors are open.

As I wandered recently through that flea market in the old mill where saddles were lined in rows, waiting for new owners, for a moment, I was back in those sweet days of childhood, Heisan and I champing at the bit to fly away.

Goodbye, Mom

"Please play 'Melody in F' again, Mom," I asked.

My mother, without hesitation, would sweep her long fingers effortlessly across the keyboard and play the Anton Rubinstein piece again for me. That is the way my mother was. Although she had already played it once, she was always generous, always willing to please. The music that flowed from our ornate, brown, turn-of-the-century upright piano in the living room of our Skowhegan home, day in and day out, is one of the things about my childhood I will remember most, long into my twilight years.

It was a sweet thing to wake in the morning to the sounds of Chopin, Bach, and Mozart wafting up the stairs and into my room, which sported dark blue wallpaper with tiny gold markings, a hardwood floor, and three windows with white ruffled curtains overlooking our driveway and barn. When Mom was older, she got hooked on Scott Joplin's music and would play it with verve, literally bouncing off the piano seat.

My mother was a jubilant person. She loved life. If there was a gathering of family or friends, she'd be the first one there and the last to leave. If we wanted to go to Marden's Surplus & Salvage store in Waterville or the coast, or even just for a ride out into the country, she was game.

When she was younger, she stood five feet, eight inches tall. She was tall, athletic, and dark haired and excelled at tennis and ping pong. She loved to swim and was extremely active. As she aged and her hair turned gray, she developed osteoporosis, and her bones sometimes broke or cracked for no reason, which was painful, but she rarely complained. By the time she was in her nineties, she had shrunk to about five feet tall and was rail thin, but her smile never wavered.

Frances Emma Rowell was born in Skowhegan and grew up the youngest of three children. Her mother was a teacher and her father, a high school principal and teacher who taught at various schools during the school year, including at Rumford and Jackman high schools, as well as at Dow Academy in Franconia, New Hampshire, where my grandfather was headmaster and was friends with the poet Robert Frost, whom my mother met. My Aunt Barbara once tied a string around Frost's finger, declaring, "This is for you to remember me by."

My mother's family lived in a lovely rural summer house in Cornville during the warm season. Her oldest brother, Gordon, attended Bowdoin College and Columbia University, and her sister, Barbara, attended Bates College. After my mother graduated, the valedictorian of Jackman High, she just assumed she would also go on to attend a good academic school. But her parents informed her that they had run out of adequate funds after financing her siblings' education, and she would have to attend nursing school.

My mother was sorely disappointed but accepted the financial reality. She went off to study at Maine Medical Center in Portland, made lifelong friends and became a skilled, hardworking, and empathetic registered nurse who worked for years at the local hospital in Skowhegan. Long after she retired, people would remark about how kind and attentive she was to them. While she was a student in nursing school, she met Edwin Ross Calder, a student at Portland School of Fine and Applied Art, at a dance. They married in 1946, and she later would give birth to seven children.

I was the youngest of the seven, and I had fifty-eight years with my mother. When she died on January 1, 2015 at age ninety-two, I knew my life would be forever changed.

They say that when you lose your mother, you lose a big part of yourself. For me, this is true.

It is shock at first, of course, although you know she is leaving and try to prepare yourself. But there really is no preparation for such a profound loss; afterward, you are faced with the task of redefining your life—trying to figure out who you are without her.

When my father died four years earlier and wanted her to go at the same time, she said, in her characteristically practical manner, "I'm not ready yet!" When a momentary twinge of guilt crept in, I assured her she had at least four more years to go—that he had lasted until ninety-two and she must, too. I think she liked that rationale.

My mother had much more to do, many more places to go, and music to play. After the initial shock of my father's death, she settled in, as did we, and adapted to life without him. Time heals, it's true. We had some fun times after that and were able to laugh and enjoy life, though in a different way. And in the void my father left, we had a focus—Mom.

We did everything we could to make her comfortable and give her the things she wanted, although she did not want for much. She was happy just to have us around her. Mom thought about death once in a while, but she wasn't afraid of it, unlike my father. Mostly, she worried about what would happen to her beloved cat, Tootsie, when she was no longer around.

"Who will take her? Where will she go? What will she do if she doesn't have all this land to run around on, the barn to chase mice in, the gardens to hide in, the trees to climb?"

I told Mom not to worry—that one of us would take her. Indeed, the Sunday before she died, my sister Jane brought Tootsie to her house to live with her two cats.

My mother was barely conscious that last week, but I got to tell her that Tootsie was fine—that she actually loved being at Jane's. My mother flinched as if to say she understood, but I couldn't tell if she approved, as Tootsie would no longer rule the roost.

I think Mom would approve now. I visit Tootsie often, and she greets me with recognition every time, seeming to know I am part of her former world with my mother. That world was a warm, comforting, safe place, where music and laughter and the scent of sweet stollen bread baking in my mother's oven would filter up the stairs to meet me in the morning. There was always something exciting happening downstairs when my mother was home, and I didn't want to miss out.

Those were happy times, in a house that is now eerily quiet. Cleaning it out these past few months has been hard—painful—yet cathartic. My mother's presence is there in every book, photo, newspaper clipping, recipe, every scrap of paper I find with her handwriting scrawled across it. Her scent is in every drawer, every piece of clothing, every banged-up pot and pan in which she baked her incredible pastries, pies, and loaves of bread.

In the now silent upstairs, I can hear her voice, her irrepressible laughter, echoing off the walls of the empty rooms—rooms that once held our dreams as we lay in beds made up with my mother's wind-dried, sun-kissed sheets.

I found a few treasures in my quest to see and touch everything in that house before it was sold. There was the dress my mother made for me in 1974 when I was a senior in high school and needed something to wear for class night. The long, flowery gown with puffy sleeves and pearl buttons was in the bottom of a trunk, all bunched up and wrinkled but in excellent shape. Unable to bear parting with it, I had it cleaned, and it now hangs on the door in our guest room, where it serves as a reminder—not only of her workmanship

Me and my mom in 2000.

but also of the generosity with which she would sew a dress, bake a cake, listen to my stories, or perform a piano piece whenever I asked.

In the maelstrom of organizing nearly sixty years' worth of accumulated household items and mementos, I also discovered four 35 mm films, only one of which was marked. It says "Florida, 1958" in my father's handwriting. I sent the films off to Las Vegas to be placed onto a DVD. A few weeks later, the DVD arrived, offering the biggest gift of all.

It is fifteen minutes of pure joy, watching my mother and father in Boca Raton more than a half-century ago, playing tennis and golf, diving into a pool, and having a grand time away from us seven rambunctious children.

They are so young and happy, bouncing up the steps of the airplane for their return flight to Maine. Like movie stars, they smile glamorously as they wave good-bye. But I know their happiness is not all about having a much-needed vacation in the sun—it is that they know they are coming home to us.

And that is the way I will remember my mother on Sunday—Mother's Day—and all the days thereafter—young, energetic, and throwing her head back in laughter.

ON THE BEAT

Return of the Native

It's funny how the decisions you make early in life with the intention of spreading your wings and exploring new territory can sometimes bring you right back to where you started.

Such was the case with me. I spent my last three summers of high school working at Camp Modin, a summer camp for boys and girls of Jewish faith on Lake George in both Skowhegan and Canaan. I worked in the kitchen as a dishwasher my first summer, a waitress my second, and an assistant cook my third.

The campers and counselors at Modin came from all over the world, but many hailed from New York and New Jersey. I was fascinated with their worldliness and sophistication and grew to love their culture. I made fast friends at Modin and kept in touch with many, long after I left Skowhegan.

I decided that after graduating from Skowhegan Area High School in 1974, I would attend a small, private college, rather than University of Maine, which a lot of students chose because it was close to home and a good school and the tuition was affordable.

I wanted to leave Maine to learn about other people and places and decided I would attend a college that was close to New York so that I could take the train down to visit my Modin friends, see Broadway shows, and explore all the city had to offer. Also, it would still be close enough to Maine so I could visit when I wanted. I settled on University of Hartford in West Hartford, Connecticut, because it fit the bill on all counts.

I was homesick during my first semester away from home. I loved my classes but wanted to come back to Maine. I applied to University of Maine at Orono, got accepted, and planned to enroll there in January of 1975. However, at Hartford, I started working as a reporter at the student newspaper, made friends, and slowly felt more at home. By Thanksgiving, I decided there was no way I was heading back to Maine.

After graduating with a bachelor's in English, I worked at various jobs in Connecticut and Massachusetts, including as an office manager for a small manufacturing company and the manager of a self-service gas station.

Through it all, working in journalism really was my dream, but I lacked the courage to apply for jobs in the field. Instead, I went back to school. I enrolled in the school of education at the University of Massachusetts at Amherst, thinking that if I became certified to teach high school English, I would always have that option to fall back on if other job efforts failed. I studied hard for a whole year, including the summer, earning all A's. During my last semester, I was a student-teacher at Frontier Regional High School in South Deerfield, Massachusetts. While I loved the students, I found teaching to be all-consuming, having to spend entire weekends and free time creating lesson plans, correcting tests, and reading and marking essays. I decided teaching was not for me.

At that point, I had been living and working away from Maine for thirteen years—I missed it and I now longed to return.

So, in the summer of 1987, I moved back to Skowhegan and took a few months off. In the spring of 1988, I saw an ad in the *Morning Sentinel* seeking a correspondent to cover the town of Norridgewock. I applied, got the job, and never looked back.

Reporting the news for nearly thirty-five years and writing a column for the last fourteen has been fun, exciting, fulfilling, and educational. I have often described it as like going to school and getting paid for it.

People have asked me if I ever aspired to leave and work at larger newspapers in major cities such as New York, and honestly, I never have. I spent a lot of time in cities when I was younger and loved exploring the arts and culture they offered, but I've never been so happy as I am right here in Maine, where the air is fresh, the countryside and coast are exquisitely beautiful, and the people hardworking and sensible. They tell the best stories, and I get to share them. I've never regretted coming back, and it is here I will stay. Maine is home.

The Empire Grill

My sister, my husband, and I took a booth at the Empire Grill. We sat by the window with a view of downtown Skowhegan on one side and the footbridge spanning the Kennebec River on the other. It was on a Saturday, the day before the Empire Grill closed for good in 2010.

The Empire Grill was a key location in the HBO movie *Empire Falls*, filmed in the early 2000s in Waterville and Skowhegan. It starred the late, great Paul Newman and was based on Maine author Richard Russo's Pulitzer Prize-winning novel of the same name. The film also starred Newman's wife, Joanne Woodward, as well as Ed Harris, Helen Hunt, Aidan Quinn, and a host of other famous actors. Much of the story revolves around the Empire Grill, which was portrayed as a local diner in a run-down Maine mill town. Miles Roby, played by

Harris, operates the grill. For the movie, an old pizzeria was renovated in 2003 to represent a vintage Maine diner and became the Empire Grill. When filming ended, the Grill stayed open in real life.

As the three of us sat in the warm and lazy atmosphere of the diner that day, memories of the time when Hollywood rolled into Waterville came flooding back:

Of the first day of filming at Bee's Snack Bar in Winslow, where I arrived early in the morning to watch a bearded and bedraggled Newman play the part of Harris' father and work his magic.

Of that chilly fall night in 2003 when I stood outside the grill with a handful of others, watching Helen Hunt rant at Ed Harris as they marched through the swinging door from the kitchen to the dining room, rehearsing a scene.

Of Hunt arriving at the Bob-In in Waterville for a scene inside "Callahan's" bar.

Of the cold November day the crew filmed a school shooting scene at Waterville Senior High School, a.k.a. Empire Falls High School.

A *Sentinel* photographer and I were covering the filming, and we were asked to jump in and play a fictional newspaper reporter and photographer who rushed to the school after the tragedy. The crew shot the scene over and over, spending nearly a whole day for a scene in which we appear for just a few seconds.

For three months, we covered the filming of *Empire Falls*. We attended the cast party when it was over. It was a fun diversion from the usual reporting fare and an education about how a movie is made, about the incredible amount of hard work that goes into it, and about the enormous number of people needed to take it from concept to screen.

The experience forever changed the way I look at films. Now, I'm always imagining the crew behind the camera. It was a magnificent experience and one we all knew at the time would not likely be repeated here any time soon.

So, as I sat with my husband and sister in the Empire Grill that weekend, watching real-life characters come and go, a line from a Robert Frost poem floated through my mind: ". . . nothing gold can stay."

Everywhere, there are reminders of that impermanence. The great Paul Newman, who I think stole the spotlight in *Empire Falls*, is now gone.

A few years after the movie, there was a sale at the former Hathaway shirt factory in Waterville where the movie was filmed, offering up furniture, clothing, lamps, paintings, and other film props. I bought an Empire Grill menu and a license plate from a van featured in the movie driven by Dennis Farina, who played the Silver Fox. People from all over Maine and beyond scooped up the rest.

Interestingly, fiction in at least one instance became reality: The film's narrator, according to Russo's script, accurately predicted that an out-of-towner would come in and convert the old shirt factory into a retail space with high-end apartments overlooking the river. And, indeed, the former Hathaway factory has been thus transformed.

Even as the final curtain was about to fall on the real-life Empire Grill, patrons imagined a rich Hollywood mogul coming into town to save the restaurant.

"It's got to be sad for the people that live here," said Susan Montell, a Gardiner woman who was visiting the grill with her family for the first time. "Maybe somebody will buy it."

But Kerry Pomelow, who co-owns the business with Tom Miller, does not hold out hope. The economy, the fact that they do not own the building, and other issues made it difficult to keep the grill afloat, she said.

"We have it on Craigslist. We own the trademark and business and everything that's not a wall. But honestly, in today's economy, I just don't see somebody coming here and paying what we put into it."

If nobody does, I ask, then what will become of the grill's contents, including the *Empire Falls* memorabilia? "We'll probably end up selling it," she said.

In years to come, we'll talk about the time the movie people came to town, and Kerry Pomelow will likely reminisce about her own dream of making a go of the Empire Grill.

But for now, she has no future plans.

"I'm going to sleep for a couple of days and let the dust settle." she said. "It's been a great adventure; it's been a great run. I love the people here. It's like a family. Everything ends, and something else begins." (March 6, 2010)

[Note: The former Empire Grill several years ago became a Thai food restaurant. It remains so today.]

Smokin' Joe Comes to Town

One of the greatest things about being a newspaper reporter is that you get to meet all sorts of people, both famous and infamous. Sometimes, it's when you least expect it.

October 14, 1992 was such a day for me.

I was working at the Skowhegan bureau of the *Morning Sentinel* and got a call from Evelyn Veilleux, owner of Evelyn's New & Used Furniture. She told me someone famous was going to arrive at her store in five minutes, and she had invited only a few friends to come by to meet him. And she said that I was the only person from the media that she was inviting.

"It's Joe Frazier," she whispered.

I couldn't quite believe my ears.

"You mean Smokin' Joe—the former world heavyweight boxing champ? At your store?"

"One and the same," she said.

I hung up the phone and looked at Betty Withee, a former reporter who was the bureau's receptionist at the time.

"Betty," I said, "either this woman is crazy or she's telling the truth. But either way, I'm not taking any chances."

I grabbed my trusty Pentax K1000 camera and flew out the door, jumped into my car, and sped up to the furniture store about a mile away on North Avenue. There were a dozen or so men hanging around outside the store in baseball caps, not saying much and just waiting. I joined them, and we spent twenty minutes or so kicking the dirt and making small talk. Pretty soon, a white stretch limousine pulled up in front of us and parked. A door opened, and out came Joe Frazier, grinning in his gray suit, black cowboy hat, multicolored tie, and gold jewelry, including a necklace with a gold crown. We were all so stunned that we couldn't speak.

Most fans converge on superstars in such circumstances, but not these Mainers. They respectfully stood there, silent, until big Joe broke the ice.

"What's happening? Nice to see you," said Frazier, who was forty-eight at the time.

I started snapping pictures, amazed that I was actually photographing the great Smokin' Joe, right here in little-old Skowhegan, Maine. I noticed his right hand was bandaged up around the wrist. Like a good reporter, I asked what happened.

"Long story," was all he said.

We went inside the store, where someone was offering to take people's pictures with him for five dollars.

Smokin' Joe was friendly, talkative, and funny. And he didn't look down on us Mainers. He certainly didn't look down at me.

"You're tall," he said, as I started asking him questions.

Smokin' Joe Frazier in 1992. Photo by Amy Calder.

As it turned out, he was at the store as part of a promotional campaign for a furniture wholesale company based in Philadelphia, where he lived. Evelyn's carried the furniture line at the time. I remember Town Manager Pat Dickey was there and got an autograph for her father, who lived in England and was a sports fan. Harold Brown, the town's deputy police chief, also was on hand. Just in case a fight broke out, someone joked. Veilleux said she was thrilled to have him at her store.

"He's just great for business!" she crooned.

I know all this, because I spent one morning, nineteen years later, rifling through my personal archives, searching for the story I wrote about Joe that day. I finally found it, nestled among other clips from 1992. The headline reads "Smokin' Joe visits Maine." Former reporter Darla Pickett covered Joe when he visited a couple in Winslow later, so she shared a byline with me.

The picture I took of Joe after he got out of the limo that day is a treasured possession. Years ago, I framed it and hung it in our sunroom, where it has been a topic of conversation over the years.

When I learned that Joe died of cancer at the age of sixty-seven, I took the photograph down and brought it to the office to share with my coworkers. We've been enjoying it and reminiscing about his fights with Muhammad Ali. Godspeed, Smokin' Joe. It was a real pleasure meeting you. (November 12, 2011)

Beards and Blaze Orange

It's October, and soon, the bearded men will come out. They'll be men you don't recognize at first, but upon closer inspection, you realize you've made a mistake. They don't don the disguise for any sinister reason; they just want to be warm when they head out into the woods and fields in this rust-colored season before the snow comes.

We will see them in blaze-orange hats and vests, trudging down rural roads, rifles at their sides. They might be alone; they might be in pairs. Chances are, they've filled their hungry bellies with a hot breakfast served up at home or in community centers, churches, and Grange halls.

These bearded men are Maine deer hunters, and they've been around a long, long time. Many count on the annual hunt to fill freezers with meat for their families. Some haul the carcasses out of the woods themselves, cut up the meat, and package it for freezing. Others let the butcher shop do the work.

Growing up in rural Maine, I saw hunting as a necessary activity for many families. Seeing a deer hanging in our barn for the first time, I decided I couldn't shoot one of those beautiful animals myself, but I wasn't going to fault anyone else who did. Hunters now include men and women, husbands and wives, sisters and brothers. In high school, we were led into the auditorium one day to see a film about deer hunting. We were told hunting was important to thin out the deer herd in Maine which, if left to increase, would mean some deer would starve.

Like my brothers, I was taught how to fire a gun, a skill that I'm glad I have, although I hope I never have to use it. When I was in junior high, we students attended Bryant Pond conservation camp, and many of us got National Rifle Association badges after successfully learning to handle and use a gun properly and safely. I value that course to this day and discovered several years ago as a guest at a bird-hunting club outing that I never lost the skill. I'm comforted to know that, if I needed to, I could grow my own food and shoot a bird or rabbit for sustenance. Shooting a deer would be harder, but I expect I could do it if I had to. I'm not a big fan of deer meat, but I'm sure I'd be darned glad to eat it if I was truly hungry.

You can take the girl out of Maine, but not Maine out of the girl, I suppose. Intellectualizing about whether it's right or wrong to kill animals for food is easier when one lives in the city, away from those who rely on this rural source of nutrition.

It's a curious thing, this pride in being a scrappy Mainer, when at heart, I'm somewhat of a pacifist and don't like to kill anything, really. I'll toss a spider or a fly out the window rather than stamp on it, shoosh away a mosquito before I'll swat it. But being an omnivore, I'm realistic, too. We've got to eat. And the Maine forests provide us with food if we need it.

Many hunters say they love getting outdoors in the crisp fall air, tramping through the quiet woods where the fir trees smell like Christmas and a dusting of snow helps mark their trail. You might give a hunter a silent wave when you see him. Whisper hello. Above all, don't forget to wear your blaze orange. (October 9, 2010)

Technology Comes to the Newsroom

When I started working as a newspaper correspondent for the *Sentinel* in 1988, I worked from home and was issued a tiny portable computer that sort of looked like a laptop except it wasn't as slim and had a little screen on which you could see only about three lines of text. Since I couldn't see much of a story on the screen, I had to remember what paragraphs I had already written so that my transitions made sense. Still, I got so proficient and fast with that thing, I could bang out a story in minutes. So, when I became a staff reporter and started working in the *Morning Sentinel* newsroom, I wondered how I'd ever get used to working on a real computer with its ominously large screen and orange type. Luckily, it didn't take long.

In my early days as a reporter, nobody had cellphones, so when I was out covering stories, I couldn't easily call an editor to update them on what was happening. However, there were times, rumbling over those old, potholed roads in Somerset County, when I really needed to contact an editor about something. To make the call, I'd stop at someone's house, knock on the door, and ask if I could use the telephone. Fortunately for me, most people were happy to oblige.

Not only didn't we have cellphones, we didn't even have a fax machine in the office. So if we needed any kind of paperwork, it had to be mailed to us. I remember once interviewing someone in California for a story and then waiting a week until some needed documents arrived in the mail.

And, of course, things kept changing, as they always do.

I was one of the first *Morning Sentinel* reporters to write a story about what would later become known as the internet. I went to a small house in Skowhegan that had been converted into an office, and I wrote a story about a young man who was excited about the phenomenon he said would become like an "information highway."

"You'll be able to send a message to someone in Russia, and he'll get in it within seconds," he said.

I think of that interview often when I look at where we are now.

Little did I know more than twenty years ago that the people who typed up press releases and delivered them to us at the office would no longer come to see us in person. These folks, who were from hospitals, civic organizations, schools, and other places, now just press a button, and we have the information at our desks almost instantly.

When email was first introduced into the *Sentinel* newsroom, the office had only one computer—located in the library off the newsroom—that was capable of sending and receiving emails. We had to wait our turns to use that computer, and it was always in demand. It's laughable to think of it now, given how much we depend on email for so many things—press releases, tips about important stories, communication with editors.

At one time, a reporter's day included numerous editorial meetings to discuss the day's stories; now, most of that discussion is done online. Editors don't need to huddle around our desks like they used to in order to jot down what we were all working on for the day.

We used to get lots of regular mail every day, too, and now, that has dwindled to practically nothing except for an occasional card or letter from a reader—usually older readers, at that. In fact, just a few months ago, we removed our personal mailbox slots, since no one got mail anymore.

I knew that the world had really changed when that happened.

My husband worked in the newsroom when reporters wrote stories on typewriters, and, after they were edited, they were retyped on hot lead machines. That was a little before my time in the newsroom, but not much. In my college journalism classes, we banged out copy on old Royal typewriters.

The changes just seem to come faster and faster. I wonder what's in store for the next twenty years? (July 9, 2011)

The Swinger of Birches

I stood in the cool parlor, staring at a photograph of Robert Frost sitting in his Morris chair next to the old coal stove. I looked back and forth from the photo to the actual scene before me—the stove to my left, a pantry of shelves and the door to the foyer. It was a strange and exhilarating sensation being in the Franconia, New

Hampshire, house where Frost lived from 1915 to 1920 and for eighteen summers thereafter.

This poet of my childhood, whose voice I can still hear reciting poems on a scratchy old record I listened to over and over, slept, ate, and wrote here. He wandered the pasture and woods, tended to animals in his barn, and slept in the bed upstairs. He wrote poetry at his desk in the parlor and, in warmer weather, on the porch overlooking the mountains.

I sat on that porch Sunday after visiting the village of Franconia and Dow Academy, where my grandfather Harold Rowell was principal many years ago and where my mother attended first and second grades. Frost often visited my grandfather there.

The academy had been transformed into condominiums, but its exterior looked much the same as it did early in the century. I spoke to a man who lives there with his family and regularly winds the old tower clock.

Frost's house on Ridge Road is now a museum and conference center that people may visit for a small donation. We were allowed to wander in the few rooms of the house open to the public. A poet-in-residence was living in the part closed off, we were told. It is a simple white farmhouse built in 1859, kept as it was in Frost's day, sparsely furnished with a few pieces from the period.

In a glass case in the parlor are some of Frost's books and letters as well as one of my favorite Frost poems, "Acquainted With the Night," written in his own hand. My heart stopped when I saw a handwritten letter from Frost to "Mr. Rowell," thinking it may have been to my grandfather, but it was not.

It was a letter to Frost's grandfather's lawyer who lived in Lawrence, Massachusetts, and who was handling the sale of the farmhouse to Frost, for just more than one thousand dollars. Frost's letter, dated May 31, 1915, urges Rowell to complete the deal.

I climbed the stairs and entered Frost's bedroom, a small room with a slanted ceiling, his bed, and one window, with an exquisite view of the mountains and blue sky. Did he dream here? I wondered. Did he wake in the night, tiptoe down the stairs while his family slept, and pen his works?

It was a hot, humid Sunday when the Poetry Society of New Hampshire was meeting in the barn. We wandered over to a trail behind the house that winds a quarter mile through the woods. Plaques bearing Frost's poetry are posted along the trail. It was cool in the woods and quiet, except for the chirping of an occasional bird and the sounds of the wind in the trees.

Back at the house, twenty-one-year-old Lily Ringler sat on the porch, writing on a laptop. A recent Dartmouth College graduate working at the Frost Place for the summer, Ringler was pleasant and accommodating.

We chatted about the house, Frost's love of the mountains, and the people who visit. I think she sensed my enthusiasm for Frost and for being there, so she relaxed house policy and gave us—my husband, Phil, and our friends John and Karol Youney—a tour of areas typically closed to the public.

The living room, with a red-painted floor, large stone fireplace, and upright piano, was adjacent to a small kitchen where Frost and his family shared meals. Upstairs, we glimpsed his children's rooms—small and simply furnished. I was delighted to discover the architecture was much like that of the house in which I grew up.

I felt privileged to be afforded a private view into the poet's life. How sweet after having spent a lifetime with his poems reverberating in my head, from the time I was too small to read right into my adulthood.

It is difficult for me now to determine where Frost's poetry stopped and reality began in my childhood. We climbed birch trees in my father's field and then rode them down to the ground, just as the narrator in the poem "Birches" did. In our playtime, we imagined being the sleigh driver in "Stopping by Woods on a Snowy Evening," a Frost poem that was the inspiration for a painting my father did that now hangs in my home. It's all mixed together in my head, Frost's poetry and my past and present life. (July 23, 2011)

Time Stood Still

On September 11, 2001, I arrived for work at the *Morning Sentinel* building on Front Street just before nine in the morning, as I did on most Tuesdays. I climbed the back stairs to the second-floor newsroom, entering through a side door near my desk. I saw what first appeared to be an empty room, as all the desks were unoccupied. I quickly understood why. Everyone was standing around a television perched on the wall across the room.

"What's going on?" I asked Stacy Blanchet, a page design editor I'd worked with for more than a dozen years.

"A plane just hit the World Trade Center in New York," she said.

I dropped my bag and joined my peers, who stood riveted to the television screen. That's when another plane hit the Twin Towers right before our eyes. I had flashbacks to the day I watched the space shuttle Challenger blow up, also on live national television, on January 28, 1986. Except that two planes crashing into the towers, one after the other, was clearly no accident.

My heart began to pound. What was going on here? We watched and listened to the news reports. We were human beings first, reporters and editors second. And then without speaking, we all knew we were in for a hectic, unpredictable day.

We started to talk about what we were going to do next as far as news coverage goes. And then a plane struck the Pentagon. It was at that moment that I got scared. If the Pentagon was hit, we were in deep trouble. Nothing like this had ever happened on American soil. I actually wondered if we would be attacked in Maine. I turned to our operations manager, longtime newsman Glenn Turner, for some assurance, barely believing what came out of my mouth next.

"Is this the beginning of World War III?" I asked.

"No," he said.

His confident response offered at least some relief.

After we began to digest what was happening, Turner started directing us reporters out into the community to talk to people and follow the events as they unfolded. Find out what they are doing, how they are feeling, what is being done locally to help them cope, he said. Try to learn what this means to us in central Maine. We all took a collective deep breath and marched out into that horrible day.

I was assigned to schools. I planned to talk to students and staff and find out how officials were dealing with the situation. I headed to Waterville Senior High School, where then-Principal Scott Phair had called an assembly in the auditorium. Students were hugging each other and crying. Staff members were doing their best to remain strong for them.

I remember feeling a deep obligation to get the news, as that was my job, but to not interfere with what school officials needed to do to help these kids and each other. I was an observer, yet I shared their fears, I shared their pain. I put on my best reporter's face and started asking questions.

Phair was good enough to let me wander the school and talk with people. I met fifteen-year-old Tabitha Soucy walking alone in the hallway. She stepped into an empty classroom, where the only sounds came from a loud television broadcasting what seemed like one terrorist attack after another.

Soucy sat down in front of the television and stared. "I'd be in lunch with the others, but I don't feel like eating," she said. "It sounds like more things are happening. It's horrible. It's scary. I'm shook up about it. My body's all shaky."

I probably did not tell her at the time, but she could have taken the words right out of my mouth. Few events in my life have had the impact on me the way 9/11 did.

I remember the assassination of John F. Kennedy on November 22, 1963. I was riding home on the school bus at age seven, and everyone around me was talking about our dead president. September 11, 2001, was like that. Time stood still. Hearts were sick. Everywhere, people sought answers.

We reporters spent the day talking with people in their most vulnerable moments as they sorted through their complex feelings of fear, anger, grief—and love for their fellow man. It was only later, after we arrived home from a long day, that we were able to start examining our own thoughts about this tragic event. It was one we hoped never to have to cover again. (September 10, 2011)

Change is the Spice of Life

It was a welcome relief to get that cool, dry air on Wednesday night, easing the irritation we've all felt for the last several days. Even our cats were looking worn out from the heat, lying on their backs on the deck with paws up in the air as if in a trance.

Sometimes they'd just look at us as if to say, "What's with this heat?"

I'm reminded of all those frigid days in January and February when we growled about the cold weather, wishing winter would end and finding solace in any glimmer of sunshine that might emerge. Like our cats, who always seem to be on the wrong side of the door, we humans surely are a fickle bunch. First, it's too hot; then, it's too cold. We get bored, but then when there's too much to do, we're overwhelmed. But a good thing about us Mainers is that we love a change of season.

After a long summer full of parties and traveling and company, we're relieved to see the tourists go, the kids go back to school, and the steamy weather dissipate. It's a time of slowing down, settling in, getting back to a sense of normalcy, and preparing for the long winter ahead.

Then we love to see the snow come, blanketing the brown earth just in time for the holidays. We hunker down, enjoying the warmth of a wood stove or fireplace. But after the wind has blown cold for weeks and the snow keeps coming down, wreaking havoc with our old bones, we long for spring. When it gets here, we can't wait for summer. Then if it's too sunny, we seek shade; too hot, we retreat to indoor air conditioning; too dry, and we pray for rain; too wet, and we want dry.

We're a peculiar breed, we New Englanders, and I think our need for and love of the changing seasons contributes to our character and lively personalities. I can't imagine living in a climate that never changes. How dull that would be! How costly and time-consuming, having to travel from a warm climate, for example, every time we wanted to go skiing. Why leave if we have the best of both worlds right here?

When I was a sophomore in high school, our English teacher, Muriel Dubuc, entered the classroom one day, smiled, and, without saying a word, wrote "Variety is the Spice of Life" on the blackboard. Then she asked us all to write an essay about the topic.

Mrs. Dubuc was one of my favorite teachers, and I pursued her directive in earnest. I don't remember what I wrote in that essay, which

I probably still have packed away somewhere, but I've never forgotten her assignment and the way she scrawled the words across the board. I loved the challenge of trying to decipher their meaning, rooting out proper examples, and finding the right words to present my case.

I'm sure our young, inexperienced minds came up with some reasonable ideas back then, but forty years later, wouldn't we hit the ball out of the park?

A lifetime of adventures has taught us that variety is, indeed, the spice of life. The more we see, do, and explore, the happier we are and the more compelling people we become. (July 21, 2012)

Do I Want My Change? Really?

I drove up to a fast food joint in Waterville the other day to grab a cup of coffee. In a hurry, I did the drive-through, ordered the coffee, and was told it cost $1.07. I approached the window, whipped out a dollar bill and a dime, handed it to the clerk, and waited.

The young man just looked at me.

"Do you want your change?" he asked.

"Huh?"

"Do you want the three cents?" he asked back.

I looked at him as if he were from Mars. "Ah, yes, please."

"OK," he said and handed me three pennies.

Am I missing something here? I know three cents is not a lot of money, but it was the first time a clerk had ever asked me if I wanted my change back. Driving away, my mind raced. I wanted to tell the boy that when I was his age, three cents meant a heck of a lot.

Back in the sixties, three cents could get you three pieces of Dubble Bubble gum, including funnies wrapped around them with waxed paper. Or in some cases, three pieces of candy per penny, which meant nine pieces altogether—a virtual steal. Maybe that clerk at the window was short three cents in his cash drawer and needed to make it up, I thought, in which case, I gladly would have given him the three cents.

I worked at a self-service gas station in Hartford, Connecticut, while working my way through college many years ago, and I was required to balance the paperwork at the end of my shift. If I was short, I had to make up the difference out of my own pocket. There were times when I'd toss in some of my own pennies if a customer was short; sometimes they even left a penny or two, saying, "Keep the change."

But I never asked a patron when he handed me a twenty dollar bill for $19.97 worth of gas if he wanted his change. It would have been tantamount to saying, "Go away. We don't give change here." And I would have been without a job the next day.

When I was a kid, old people often said that we of the younger generation didn't appreciate the value of a dollar. In the 1920s, you could buy a loaf of bread or a newspaper for just a few cents, they said. Imagine the reaction a sales clerk would get back then if he asked a customer whether he wanted his change.

As my mind tried to wrap itself around the fast-food clerk's comment, I imagined his reasons for asking if I wanted my change. Maybe he collects coins and is interested in finding some real old pennies to add to his collection? If so, I can understand that. My husband collected coins when he was a child and found it fun and interesting, so I'd gladly give that clerk all my pennies if he had asked.

Have you ever noticed how you often see pennies lying on the ground as if they were litter, with people just disregarding and stepping all over them? If someone were to travel to every town in America and collect all the discarded pennies, he might actually become rich.

Do I sound like an old penny pincher? Well, in my college days, I was. I'd collect pennies in a big jar for months until it was full. Then, I'd fetch penny rolls from the bank, roll the coins, and trade them in for bills—sometimes as much as ten dollars per load. And back then, ten dollars was a lot of money.

Anyway, back to that sales clerk.

It wasn't so much the number of pennies I was owed that bothered me as the fact that the clerk asked if I wanted them. Do businesses now train young workers to ask customers if they want their change?

The irony of all ironies—my sister and I enlisted my husband to fetch us some ice cream from a local vendor last week when we were in Skowhegan. He returned moments later with a story that sounded eerily familiar.

"I gave the woman ten dollars and was supposed to get sixteen cents back, but she asked if I would take fifteen rather than sixteen," he said.

Seriously? Twice in one week? I'm beginning to think I live in the twilight zone. (September 10, 2012)

All Signs Point to Autumn

My cucumber vines and tomato plants have been pulled, the garden cleaned up, the flowers weeded, and the lawn furniture put away. The wood is stacked in the backyard, the solar lights removed, and the lawn mowed, likely for the last time. On our front step, there's a pumpkin and a pot with fall plantings. When our black cat, Pip, passes by, we are reminded that Halloween isn't far behind. All of which is to say that summer is over. The nights are getting cold, the sky darker earlier.

My husband likes to recite to me just how many minutes of daylight we've lost. In springtime, he declares how many we've gained and how late the sun will go down. We're sad to see the summer go but relieved to feel the world calming down, summer traffic easing, and things getting back to normal.

Pip claws the bureau at six every morning like clockwork, expecting we'll spring him, but he also knows we don't let him out when it's dark, so he's confused. Another one of our cats, Bitsy, his sister, is a tiny coon cat who never takes such drastic measures to get attention, follows him to the kitchen door, waiting.

"You know it's too early," I tell them.

They stare back, perched identically side by side, then follow me back into the living room.

I tear up an old newspaper into little balls, toss them into the fireplace insert, top them with dry branches Phil collected last year from the backyard, and strike a long match. There's nothing quite as soothing as a fire on a chilly fall morning, slowly easing its warmth into the room and sending with it the faint scent of wood smoke.

The cats, now at my side, watch each movement intently. We sit for a while as I tend the fire, and eventually, they topple over and lie on their backs with paws in the air. The heat turns them comatose. They stretch, with Pip's incredibly long body reaching from hearth to coffee table.

Feeling like a mother whose kids finally are napping, I slip into the kitchen, pour dry cereal into a bowl, slice half a banana on top, and douse it with milk. Back in the living room, I pick up the newspaper and read as I eat. The sound of my spoon in the bowl jolts Pip and Bitsy awake, and they're suddenly all over me. By this time, it's light outside, and we all get a reprieve. Out they go, and finally, there's peace.

Later, after they've been out in the cold long enough, I call them, and they come bolting in, meowing and making a beeline for any human in sight. They wrap themselves around legs, jump onto chairs, and follow us from room to room, purring with happiness. Then, like clockwork, they get sleepy again. Don't cats typically sleep eighteen out of twenty-four hours? They've got the right idea; no stress there. Just watching them curl their furry bodies into a ball, content, makes me want to stay home, but I've got places to go and things to do.

"You be good cats," I say, as I slip out the door. "I'll see you later."

I like my simple routine in these early, cool autumn days that portend winter. In the quiet darkness, there's time to be still, to digest the rush and passing of summer and contemplate the upcoming season. I never tire of the ritual—the cleaning up, the battening down, and the putting away.

While it's the same rite of passage every year, each time, it feels entirely new. (October 1, 2012)

Lake George Regional Park

If you ask me what my favorite place on Earth is, I'd have to say, hands down, that it's Lake George Regional Park. I don't say this lightly. Having grown up in Skowhegan and spent many lazy, hot summer days swimming in the clear, cold water of the lake, I have fond memories and a deep attachment for the lake that goes beyond words.

When I was a teenager, I got my first summer job washing dishes at Camp Modin, which occupied both the west side of the lake in Skowhegan, known as the girls' side, and the east or Canaan side, known as the boys' side. I lived in the boys' side dining hall, overlooking the lake in a room on the second floor where kitchen and stable crews were housed.

I earned thirty-two dollars a week—a good chunk of change for a first job that also included free room and board—and I learned a whole lot about kitchen work, teamwork, and being a good employee. I also made friends from all over the world, learned a lot about and relished everything about the rich Jewish culture, and expanded my horizons beyond small-town Maine.

I loved it so much that I returned for a second summer and then a third. The third and last summer, I ran the kitchen on the girls' side and lived upstairs over the dining hall, which was on a small island and has since been razed.

I kept in touch with my Modin friends, visiting them in New York City after I went off to college in Connecticut. We saw Broadway shows, spent weekends together on Long Island, and had lots of fun reminiscing about Modin.

Many years later, after returning to Maine, I wrote newspaper stories about the eventual closing of Camp Modin on Lake George and its move to Salmon Lake in Oakland.

After the camp's exodus in 1992, the beautiful Modin property on Lake George could have been gobbled up by hungry developers had it not been for two forward-thinking women and a landowner who was determined to ensure its protection.

Modin owner David Adler met me at the Skowhegan side of the lake one day and told me he was looking for a buyer, but he refused to let the land go to someone who would develop and destroy it. Around the same time, Louise Townsend of Canaan also called me and asked if I could keep a secret. She and Kathy Peatman (now Perelka), also of Canaan, were devising a plan to get the state to buy the Modin property as a way to protect it and keep it for central Mainers to enjoy for a long time. I agreed to keep the plans under wraps, barely able to contain my excitement.

After a lot of hard work and tricky negotiations, dreams became reality. The state bought the property and agreed to lease it to the towns of Canaan and Skowhegan, which formed a nonprofit corporation to run the park. Nancy Warren became the park's first director; Bob Hubbard was the first park ranger. And thanks to a lot of hardworking, determined, loving, caring people, the park is a beautiful gem, still operating decades later.

I stopped by there on a Sunday in 2012 and walked, alone, along the east side shore where campers once jumped off the long dock into the water, swam and paddled canoes, and, on Friday evenings, celebrated the Sabbath on the grassy point facing north. The park, awash in autumn color, was lovelier than ever, the water so clear and pristine I could see right down to the bottom, just as I could all those years ago. (October 8, 2012)

The Original Social Media

Some people think I write entirely too many Christmas cards. I disagree.

I don't think 142 cards is too many. I love writing, sending, delivering, and handing out cards to my friends and family. It's something I've done all my life. It's a joy to sit down in the evening, look at my list of cards sent and received last year, and begin.

Typically, I have three or four boxes of cards and choose a card I think most appropriate for the recipient and one he or she will most likely appreciate. Giving Christmas cards is like giving little gifts to people I care about. Albeit small, the gift is personal and from the heart.

I write a lot in some cards, not so much in others. I try not to go on too long but to dispense just enough information to let people know what our year has been like, what is going on in our families, and what is coming in the new year. And, of course, I ask how the recipient is doing.

Sending Christmas cards, for me, is like being on Facebook, except you can keep in touch with people in a real-life way and produce a little gift that they can hold in their hands, not one they view in cyberspace. The great thing is, when you send cards, you receive them. And my husband and I rarely receive two identical cards, so every time we open an envelope, we get a little surprise.

My cousin Mary, who grew up in New York City but now lives in Montreal, has always been my role model when it comes to Christmas cards. For years, she has sent beautiful, artful, and tasteful cards. A long time ago, I followed her lead and have tried to find cards that are unusual and artsy.

Shopping for Christmas cards is fun for me. I make it a mission. I get an adrenaline rush when I find just the right design. Sound crazy? Maybe. But writing notes is in my blood. My grandmother taught us long ago that you should always send thank you notes when you get gifts and say something specific about them.

And when someone is in the hospital or sick, you send a card: if someone dies, a sympathy card. And don't just sign your name. Say something meaningful. I get this vein of thinking. I've had my share of serious illness and hospitalizations, where getting cards was a lifeline. We all have experienced the loss of friends and family members and know just how precious cards bearing thoughtful and heartfelt words can be.

Years ago, Earl Seidman, a very astute professor in the school of education at the University of Massachusetts at Amherst, imparted some words of wisdom I have never forgotten. He said that when you send a note or craft an essay or tell a story in writing, it is the ultimate gift, as you are giving something of yourself, from your heart. It's very easy to go out and purchase expensive presents and gift cards; it's a little more work, and challenging, to give a part of yourself.

When we were kids, we loved to see the mailman come at Christmastime because we were delighted to see all the pretty cards and read the notes inside. It was like connecting with all our friends and family around the globe in one fell swoop.

We would tack those cards up all along the archway between our dining and living rooms so we could admire and read them all during the holiday season. When illuminated by the lights of the Christmas tree, they seemed all the more magical.

All these years later, my heart skips a beat when I come home from work and see Christmas mail on the kitchen table. We savor every word, every pretty scene of reindeer on snow, of Santa Claus, the manger, and evergreens with holly. These are the truly luxurious gifts that make our Christmas complete. (December 16, 2012)

My Niece and the Skowhegan Fair

How I wish my grandniece Mina was here so I could take her to the Skowhegan State Fair again.

When Mina was seven, my sister Jane and I accompanied her to the fair. Mina lives in the French Alps and had never been to a fair before, so she was excited. Watching her skip along the midway, enthralled by all the rides, games, and glitter, was lots of fun.

We spoiled her. We bought her a pair of pink rabbit ears with battery-operated lights that flashed on and off. She wore the ears on her head like a headband and looked so beautiful with her dark hair and eyes. We also got her a necklace and bracelet and just about anything else she wanted, because soon she would be going back to France, and we wanted to go overboard in heaping on the love and affection.

Mina is a very smart little girl, and she speaks with a lovely French accent that is so endearing that I have saved her voice messages on my telephone answering machine. She loves America, and I'm sure part of the reason for that is because we have the Skowhegan State Fair.

It was a deliriously exciting place for her. She skipped alongside the pens of little ponies and pigs and llamas and exquisite birds perched in the mini farmyard and loved seeing all the dairy cows in their stalls, munching on fragrant hay and chewing their cuds. We perused the 4-H club exhibits and inspected all the garden vegetables, canned pickles and jams, cookies, cakes, breads, and other goodies. We also checked out the photography exhibit. Mina reminded me to find my friend Karol's photo of a boat, which won first prize.

We listened to a country music band playing on a stage in a small courtyard, watched the racehorses pace around a dusty track, and inhaled the great, omnipresent scent of freshly fried dough, French fries, and cotton candy.

Mina tried to get us to go on some of those terrifying rides that catapult you into the air, turn you upside down, and make you scream, but we would have none of it. At my age, I couldn't even find the courage to go on the Ferris wheel; although when I was Mina's age, I considered the Ferris wheel baby's play.

I acquiesced and agreed to go on the giant slide with Mina. We climbed what seemed like one hundred stairs to the top of the slide where we plopped down on grain sacks, threw our arms in the air, and shoved off, flying down, down, down until we landed in a heap on the ground. Mina persuaded me to do this over and over again until even she tired of it and went on to something else.

We tackled the maze of the glass house. At this, Mina was proficient. She scooted back and forth, always finding the correct turn that would ultimately steer us to the top of the house where we escaped on a winding slide that sent us flying to the ground.

She would not go on the merry-go-round; I don't know why. That would have been my first choice. It always was when I was her age. I also was partial to the Merry Mixer, a ride that went fast and tossed us around like egg beaters; the bumper cars, which made me feel grown up; and, of course, the roller coaster.

As August wends its way forward, the air turns chilly in the evenings, and the Skowhegan State Fair arrives, I think of Mina and wish she were here. I also recall my own childhood, collecting coins in a glass jar all year in anticipation of the fair's arrival, planning my course of action for when I got there, and dreaming about cotton candy and candied apples. And finally, blessedly, the day would arrive, and we got to march through those big fair gates onto the giant midway. For one spectacular day a year, we lived in a great whirling fantasy world, all color and magic and sweet treats unlike anything we experienced in our daily lives. (August 11, 2013)

Watch for Deer

My father taught me two things about driving when I was a teenager that have stuck with me and served me well over the years. One: if someone in front of you starts driving erratically, back way off, and keep your distance. Two: when you are driving at night, particularly in a rural area, scan the sides of the road constantly, back and forth, and watch for deer. If one crosses your path, expect another one to be right behind it.

It's kind of like the advice my high school driver's ed teacher gave me—when you see a ball roll into the road, expect a child to be chasing it. These vital pieces of advice come back to me now, as I'm hearing more and more people say they nearly hit a deer. While being vigilant has saved me from collisions many times, the reality is that sometimes, there's just nothing you can do to prevent it.

Years ago, I struck a deer late one night while driving on West Ridge Road in Cornville. It was during the days when we newspaper reporters had very late deadlines, so driving at midnight wasn't unusual. A deer ran out of the woods and into the narrow road. I tried to swerve to avoid it, to no avail. The thud against the grill and flying fur in the headlights was frightening. It was a terrible feeling.

The poor deer hobbled off into the woods as I pulled to the side of the road and into a nearby driveway. I could find no sign of the deer, which gave me hope it wasn't hurt too badly and would survive. With a flashlight, I inspected the damage, which turned out to be a twisted grill stuffed with deer fur. Only after a visit the next day to the auto repair shop did I learn I needed a new radiator.

Right after the accident, I was lucky to have found a house with the lights on and even luckier that the kind woman invited me in and let me use her phone to call the sheriff's department. We did not have cellphones in those days. Fortunately, my car was driveable and needed minimal repair. Other people aren't so lucky. A moose struck a coworker's car one night many years ago, totaling the car and sending my critically injured photographer colleague David Leaming to the hospital via helicopter. Fortunately, he survived, but it was a long recovery.

We really need to be mindful of wild animals as the cool air sets in, hunting season approaches, and deer are running. Expecting them to be out there should be as much a part of our consciousness as tying our shoes in the morning. I was talking recently with Waterville Police Officer Steve Brame about car-deer accidents, and he agreed that it can happen to anyone. In August, he was driving to work early one morning on Garland Road in Winslow, and a deer suddenly appeared and ran into the road, he said.

"I was able to react in time, and the deer continued running. But they can come out from behind bushes at a dead run, and you won't even have time to react. You don't know what's chasing it or what caused it to run. You've just got to stay alert and do the best you can," he said.

He advised slowing down, especially at dawn and dusk.

"The faster you speed, the lower your reaction time," he said.

Duane Brunell, safety performance analysis manager at the department's safety office, said fall is the season of the greatest deer presence, and vehicle collisions with large animals occur more frequently at night.

He advises that if you are unable to avoid such a collision, apply your brakes, let up on them just before impact, try to hit the tail end of the animal, and if possible, duck to minimize injury. I believe that this, combined with my father's words of wisdom, make for some darned good advice. (September 29, 2013)

Paying Back an Old Kindness

I admit it—I'm a sucker for saying "yes" when store clerks ask if I want to donate money to this or that.

"Do you want to donate a dollar for hurricane victims today?"

"Would you like to give to the children of our military men and women?"

"Can I interest you in contributing to the children's cancer program?"

My immediate answer, typically, is "sure," and I pull out the dollar bill.

If I feel initially irritated at being asked—as the asking seems to be happening more and more these days—it takes only a few seconds for me to reason that there is a great need out there, and those of us who can help, should help.

We must count our blessings, and I don't mean that, necessarily, in a religious sense. We need only look back on all the times others have helped us in the past to handily dole out a buck here and there to someone needing assistance. I can't add up all the times I've interviewed people who help those less fortunate and their response to my question "Why?" has been: "The community has been good to me, and this is my way of giving back."

Now, my husband, who would be the first to take in a hungry person and feed him, flinches every time I say "Sure" to those store clerks or others collecting money for a cause. It's not that he's stingy; I think it's that he is more conservative than I and would say, perhaps, "Can you give to every other charity, instead of every one?"

Recently, we stopped at our favorite gas station to fill up. It was Sunday night, the time I usually buy gas for the week. As I was whipping out my debit card, I heard a strong but somewhat forlorn voice asking a woman pumping gas if she could spare a couple of dollars for gasoline—just enough to get him to Waterville, where he lives.

"I got here and realized I left my wallet home," he said.

I looked back and saw a young man, probably in his twenties, standing next to a black car parked at the tank. Without taking time to intellectualize, I reached into my wallet, took out a five dollar bill, and handed it to him.

"Oh, thank you," he said, clasping his hands together in a gesture of gratitude.

Then, he held out his hand.

"My name's Mike," he said.

"I'm Amy," I replied.

My husband finished filling the tank, and we got back into the car; he, mercifully, did not press me except to ask how much I gave the guy.

"Just five dollars," I said.

Then I told him a story about the time in college when I was stranded outside Hartford, Connecticut, heading back to school from Skowhegan in the middle of the night (I preferred nighttime driving to avoid traffic jams and aggressive city drivers). I was nineteen and poor as a church mouse, with just enough cash to get me back to the city and into the campus dining hall for a pre-paid meal.

Somehow, I got lost, some twenty-five or so miles away from Hartford. It was dark, late, and scary, being out in the middle of nowhere. The more I drove around trying to find my way, the more lost I became, and I was getting dangerously low on gas.

I pulled over to check a map, and shortly thereafter, an older man stopped his car to see if I needed help. I sensed he meant well and told him my story. He plucked a twenty dollar bill and a five dollar bill from his pocket and handed them to me, gave me directions to the nearest all-night gas station, and wished me well. I asked for his name and address so I could pay him back, but he declined, walked to his car, and drove off.

While I have never forgotten that act of kindness, I honestly did not think of it until Sunday night, after we pumped gas and got back into the car to drive home.

"Sometimes an opportunity presents itself," I told my husband, "and you just know you must oblige." (August 10, 2014)

Studded Snow Tires

On October 1—the day we may legally don our studded tires—I will be doing so. When the snow tires go on, you all know what that means. Winter is not far behind.

I normally would not put them on so early in the season, but I had to make a decision. My car needs new tires now. Shall I buy them, put them on the car for only a month or two, and then replace them with studded snows or simply put the snows on now and buy new summer tires next spring?

The latter seems more reasonable.

This may not actually be jumping the gun, my putting the studded snows on early. They say we are in for a horrid winter this year—cold, snowy, and brutal. A white Halloween, white Thanksgiving, and white Christmas is what I heard someone say we're in for, and I don't mind that a bit.

I love snow; it's the ice that wreaks havoc on my sanity in winter. There's nothing worse than slip-sliding around on icy roads, out of control, heart pounding, and with no power to curb the errant vehicle. At least with snow, we can head into a snowbank if push comes to shove.

It seems to me that the ice came particularly early last winter, and it was pure aggravation from the start. It also was the first time in my life that I declared "Enough of this nonsense" and bought studded snow tires. For many years before that, I'd prided myself on never having to buy snow tires because I was such a good driver and, being a hardy Mainer, could handle any road conditions just fine. Beyond that, I reasoned, I saved lots of cash over the years using only all-season radials.

But as I grow older, I stop trying and pretending to be so stalwart. If I'm cold, I turn up the heat. If I happen to be craving something sweet, I reach for something sinful and vow to harbor no guilt about it.

A few years ago, I swallowed my pride and bought a remote starter for my car. Every day for many years, I passed the shop that sells and installs them and, one day, stopped and made the remote starter my Christmas present. I have not regretted that decision one single minute.

How nice it is to get into a warm car at twenty below zero. It may be a poor use of fuel, but hopefully, never again will I have to throw hot water on my door locks to unfreeze them when the stupid de-icing spray doesn't work. I figure there are certain things we earn as we age, and warm toes and fingers at all times are some of those.

When I was out early last winter in an ice storm, flailing around on the roads like a runaway train, I decided to relinquish all claim to invincibility and join the ranks of sensible people who use studded snow tires.

My little car drove more like a truck with the studded snows. Yes, the click, click, click of the studs on pavement was annoying at first, but I got used to it real quick. The tires did not work perfectly in all winter conditions, but they were a darned sight better than those I'd hobbled through winters with for most of my life. And at least I could leave the house in the mornings without fear of always slamming into the car in front of me.

Yes, winter is coming, and we'd better embrace it, as there's not much of an alternative. For me, that means making it a bit more palatable by using every trick in the book. (September 28, 2014)

How High is Your Snow?

We do peculiar things, we Mainers, as the snow continues to wrap around us, squeezing us out of house and home—and our sanity. Cabin fever is real. We wander from room to room, muttering to ourselves. We clean out closets and cabinets and rearrange dishes on shelves. As the snow kept piling itself higher and higher on our roof last week and people began to panic about too much weight on roofs, we started to fidget.

Years ago, my husband and I sold our roof rake at a lawn sale, thinking we'd never need it again. With global warming and the winters becoming less severe, surely we'd not have to worry. But this winter proved us wrong.

Watching three feet of snow on the south side of our roof turn into four and five feet, we began to ponder the possibility that one night, we'd hear a giant roar and feel a great gust of wind blow into our living room as all the snow would come crashing down onto our napping felines.

"You haven't shoveled your roof?" a colleague asked me in disbelief.

I went home and told my husband we might want to get the roof shoveled. When our friend Dave came to visit one day, Phil asked if he could borrow his roof rake.

"Sure, I'll bring it over, but I think you need your own rake," was the reply.

A couple of days later, Dave told me he'd scout out roof rakes at hardware stores and buy one if I approved, which I did. I seriously doubted they'd have any in stock, but he scored, finding me one for fifty-nine dollars.

When I delivered the rake to Phil, he seemed not to react much. I attributed it to the price, as the last time he bought one, thirty years ago, it was only thirty dollars. Just then, our contractor called to say that while he was in Florida, he had a crew that could come and shovel the snow off our roof for a good deal if we wanted.

"Oh no," I said, "We bought a roof rake and plan to do it ourselves."

He tried to discourage me. He said he's twenty-five years younger than we are and pretty rugged, and even he has trouble wrangling a roof rake in this kind of snow. Our contractor has never steered us wrong, but I declined, thanked him, and told him to enjoy all that sun.

Come Saturday morning, with more snow in the forecast, we donned our arctic gear and headed to the backyard where Phil promptly started raking the porch roof from the deck. It worked well, and we were psyched.

But raking the house roof itself, a feat that required that we perch ourselves chest deep in snow, was another story. Undeterred, however, I hoisted the rake up onto the roof and started methodically scraping downward. It took barely twenty minutes of whacking the snow, scraping and flailing around in several feet of snow myself, before I concluded roof raking was not my forte. Winded, cold, and fearing I might have a heart attack, I declared to Phil that we'd better call our contractor.

"We're too old for this," I said.

Phil conceded he never intended to rake the roof at all. The blank look on his face when I presented the new rake to him was a result of his figuring that, if he asked to borrow Dave's rake, Dave would bring it over and rake the roof himself. Phil didn't plan on actually buying a new one.

I dialed up our contractor, who lay poolside in sunny Florida.

"Can you send your crew 'round?" I asked, meekly.

I could hear the "I told you so" in his voice as he promised to get someone there by Monday. Relieved and satisfied that we had made the right decision, we arrived home from errands Monday evening to find the roof black instead of white, piles of snow around the house where earlier there had been none, and two cats—who normally greet us yawning and stretching—looking stunned and annoyed.

But, hey, we learned our lesson; when the raking gets tough, the tough call a contractor. (February 22, 2015)

Remember Encyclopedias?

I never thought I'd live to see the day that the phone book became obsolete.

In the old days of newspapering, it was invaluable. We never threw out phone books in the newsroom of the eighties and nineties. If we couldn't find a phone number in the newest phone book, we'd look in an older one and, more often than not, find what we needed. And if not, we'd consult an even older one.

I used to keep a phone book everywhere—at home, in my car, on my desk; it was probably one of the more important reference books in my collection. Not anymore.

And remember encyclopedias?

Talk about reference books. When we were kids, we did our homework in the closest proximity to encyclopedias as we could. It was the same with the dictionary and thesaurus. They were important when we were kids, even more so when we became college students.

I don't remember exactly when my Webster's dictionary and Roget's thesaurus got moved from a prominent place on my office desk within easy reach to a more remote location with less important things, such as the world atlas and a Maine map. But they did get moved over time, ever so subtly and by my own hand.

First, they were right in front of me, where I could pluck them up quickly, flip through their pages, and pinpoint what I needed. Over time, they'd become worn and torn and yellowed until it was time to buy updated versions. Eventually, as the internet proved more user-friendly and convenient than books, I relegated the dictionary and thesaurus to my lower left desk drawer—again without major decision-making or fanfare.

And the atlas and Maine map? Long gone, in this age of internet and GPS.

I open my desk drawer today and find the latest edition of *The Associated Press Stylebook*, a 1902 version of the hardcover book *The Centennial History of Waterville*, and a tiny Newspaper Guild handbook; and there, tucked in the side of the drawer, are the *Merriam-Webster Dictionary* with a 1997 copyright, and *The Concise Roget's International Thesaurus, Revised and Updated Sixth Edition*—copyright 2003.

While obviously I no longer need either, I believe I keep them there for—what reason?

Maybe to remind me of where I came from, a time before I had not one but two computer screens on my desk—one to write my stories on and the other to write emails, check Facebook and Twitter, post my stories, check the newspaper's website, access the electronic archives, and, yes, search for historical records, people, places, and words—all those things I used to get from the dictionary, thesaurus, atlas, maps, encyclopedia, and other reference materials.

I've no doubt that, one day, my dictionary and thesaurus will disappear from my drawer, as will the paper files I've been keeping there just in case the whole computer world blows up, so I can tell younger reporters, "I told you so."

But those four Waterville phone books dating back to 2007 that I keep on my desk aren't going anywhere. Granted, they are to the far left of my desk calendar, which I suppose I don't need anymore, and behind a tray holding my blank expense sheets, which will soon become unnecessary because we are going to be doing them electronically—and a few sheets of *Morning Sentinel* stationery and envelopes, which I seldom use anymore.

But I refuse to relegate those phone books to my desk drawer, even though the telephone company says future phone books will not contain residential white page listings. Those will be available only upon request. (March 22, 2015)

The Joy of Maine Stores

We whizzed along Route 32 in Windsor, approaching Hussey's General Store, which advertises guns, wedding gowns, and cold beer.

"Have you ever been to Hussey's?" I called to Evalyn Bowman, who was in the back seat. She never had, so I insisted we stop.

Evalyn is my good friend who is seventy-nine and has more energy than all four of us in the car that day, including my husband, Phil, and sister Jane. We were headed to the coast to show Evalyn the Pemaquid Point Lighthouse, have lobster at Shaw's Wharf in New Harbor, and take a side trip to Round Pond.

Evalyn was enthralled with Hussey's and said she was going to go back there to shop one day. The store, which has only improved with age, carries everything from wood stoves to groceries, as well as new and used books.

When I was a girl growing up in Skowhegan, my Aunt Barbara and Uncle Carl Kirkpatrick lived in Windsor and always bought our Christmas gifts at Hussey's. I remember being amazed, at age twelve, that a classy navy blue and white sweater could come from a general store in a small town.

On our trip to the coast, Evalyn ran around Hussey's, admiring the kitchen stuff, blue glassware—which she collects—greeting cards, and food on the first floor; clothing, guns, and an entire bridal department on the second; and hardware in the basement.

I bought a carbon monoxide detector, perused the shelves of paint, eyed the copper weathervanes perched by the staircase, and insisted Evalyn climb onto the Big Daddy fold-up chair near the camping gear so I could snap a picture.

A petite woman, Evalyn needed a footstool to get onto the chair, which was three times the size of a normal one. The store clerk, enjoying our plans for a photo shoot, happily retrieved a footstool, and there Evalyn sat in the giant chair, grinning for the camera.

We in Maine are lucky to have stores like Hussey's, Renys, and Marden's Surplus & Salvage, which provide us with just about everything we need to survive in this state, all in one store. Where else except at a Renys store can you buy a pair of Carhartts for half price and nab a handful of tennis shirts for three bucks apiece on the next rack? And in a nearby aisle find hoes, rakes, dishes, and gourmet chocolate?

At Marden's, where they tell you you should have bought it when you saw it, you can furnish your entire house, as well as your kitchen cupboards. They've got sofas and carpets, dining room and bedroom sets, shoes, groceries, and fifty-cent greeting cards, not to mention nails and screws by the pound, books, and lawn furniture. I'm forever kicking myself when I visit Jane's house and sit under her sturdy blue patio umbrella that she bought at Marden's a few years ago for thirty dollars that I didn't buy one too when I saw it.

The thing about these stores is that they always have new stuff, so visiting one is as much a treasure hunt as it is a foray into finding something you need at a decent price. And you never know what you're going to find there. A few years ago, for instance, Marden's had a whole display of real stuffed bears and other animals for sale. Not kidding.

For my friends who visit from out of state, Marden's and Renys are a must-stop and rank right up there with the Colby Museum of Art. The stores are doing something right in their ability to understand what we Mainers want and need at a price that doesn't break our pocketbooks.

It may sound funny to people from away, but the businesses also provide us with much-needed entertainment during the dark winter months when there's not much to do except stoke the fires and watch the snow come down. What happens when it's twenty below with no sun in sight? The stores' parking lots are full.

I remember years ago perusing the aisles at Renys in Madison and running into the elder Bob Reny, gone several years now. He bore a large smile as he chatted informally with customers, genuinely interested in who they were and what they were looking for. His gentle nature spoke volumes. And Mickey Marden, also gone, was a familiar, friendly figure at his Waterville store, always happy to engage patrons.

These family-owned Maine businesses and how they operate, in my opinion, are part of what makes Maine so special. And the endearing thing is they don't try to be charming; they just are.

(August 30, 2015)

Sugary Treats and Journalism

I have been gradually removing all the sugary holiday treats from the house: cookies, candy, chocolates, and cakes. The newsroom is a good place to relocate such foods, as they tend to disappear rather quickly. Traditionally, this has been so.

Anyone with leftover Christmas, Valentine's, Easter, or Halloween goodies need only drop them on the round table in the middle of the newsroom to be assured they will not be wasted. There's something about an impending deadline that brings out the sugar cravings in a good writer or editor.

If I had to guess why, the reason would have something to do with adrenaline. The closer the deadline, the more furiously we work. The more important the news, the more sugar we consume. It seems to feed the fire. That goes for salt, too. Potato chips and nuts are good fodder for a late-breaking story, as is coffee.

In the old days, cigarettes were part of that mix. I remember when the newsroom was blue with cigarette smoke, ashtrays overflowing on desks and editors running around with cigarettes dangling from their lips. Some editors kept bottles of liquor in their desk drawers, too, but that was a better-kept secret. That was years ago, of course.

While we news junkies have mended our ways when it comes to smoking in newsrooms, even the most health-conscious journalists will succumb to a prettily frosted cookie, homemade fudge, leftover apple pie, or contributed box of Russell Stover candies.

We have this thing about birthdays, too. Everyone gets a birthday cake, usually an ice cream cake from Dairy Queen. In that respect, it's fortunate that many of our birthdays fall during the spring and summer months.

This is how dedicated we are to securing cakes for our birthdays:

One day, I got a desperate call from David Leaming, a photographer who typically collects the cake from Dairy Queen. But on this particular hot summer day, he had driven his motorcycle to work. He tried to transport the cake from Dairy Queen to the office on said motorcycle, and while en route, the plastic cover blew off the cake, which landed squarely on his face and shirt. He pulled over and rushed, cake in hand, into the first building he could find, which was a medical supply company. He asked if they had a refrigerator, to which they replied that they did, and he deposited the mangled cake there until I arrived to rescue both him and it.

As I drove into the parking lot, I could see two men behind the glass doors laughing as our photographer plucked the cake from the fridge and bolted through the doors, whipped cream frosting smeared on his cheeks and clothes. By the time we got back to the office, the cake was a disaster but tasted good nevertheless.

As the holidays begin to fade away, sweets have been appearing on that newsroom table. Yesterday, it was frosted chocolate Christmas tree cakes with candy cane trunks. Today, it was a large plate of gourmet chocolate chip and mint cookies, as well as white chocolate truffle candies—all of which disappeared in less than two hours.

I was pretty health conscious, food-wise, through much of 2015, only rarely having a sweet treat, and then the holidays arrived, laying waste to all my good intentions. But as each new year is forgiving, allowing us to repair our transgressions, we may mend our ways in 2016—at least until the next holiday rolls around.

Until then, I'm going to try to do what that nice fellow on public television said the other night about foods we should and should not eat. He advised we shop the perimeter of the grocery store, ignoring the processed food in the middle, and eat a plant-based diet.

While I could argue that sugar cane is plant-based, I'll just vow to resist the temptation. (January 10, 2016)

People who Snap Gum! Arggh!

My colleagues and I got to talking about things that irk us.

We recalled a couple of former coworkers who had the habit of clipping their nails at their desks. We wondered how perfectly educated, seemingly mannered people do such things. Then, we recalled a coworker who tended to eat nuts and raw carrots all the time, which, admittedly, drove us all crazy.

The more we talked about pet peeves, the more we identified.

Gum chewing and particularly gum snapping is intolerable, we all agreed. Flossing teeth in public, sneezing without covering one's mouth, and eating potato chips with one's mouth open were at the top of our list of pet peeves. People who talk all the time without stopping to listen, those who are self-centered, and dinner hosts who help themselves to food before serving guests were also among our greatest dislikes.

Besides those irritable, annoying traits people display at inopportune times, there are those things that are harder to escape and border on being just plain inconsiderate. Shooting fireworks off, for instance, more than is necessary.

On the Fourth of July, we all expect fireworks and can even enjoy them as a visible display and celebration of our loyalty to country and independence. But firing them off on beautiful, serene summer nights when we have our windows open to listen to the loon calls on the lake or hear the wind whispering through the trees or the sound of raindrops on the roof is not at all palatable. Also not fun is watching our pets running for cover, frightened and stressed out by the noise, cowering in corners. And the loons—what must they be feeling?

Whenever I hear fireworks, whether from being woken up by the noise or sitting and waiting for them to end, I think of all the military veterans, particularly those suffering from post-traumatic stress, and how they must be affected by the rapid-fire sound of pop, pop, pop. One of my neighbors, a doctor, has spent time overseas patching up soldiers wounded in action. How must he feel? I have not asked him, but I suspect it's something he wishes he'd rather not have to hear while in the safe, secure venue of home.

Speaking of noise, there's nothing quite so irritating as being in traffic and hearing the boom, boom, boom of loud speakers from a nearby vehicle or the rumble and roar of loud motorcycle pipes (sorry bikers). In all fairness, many motorcyclists have toned down the volume.

Then there are those irritants that we really can't do anything about and with which we put up, because they have certain benefits. Driving by a paper mill that is emitting a foul odor isn't the most pleasant experience nor is the sudden, noxious scent of a skunk that has sprayed near an open window or the nasal assault we face when driving past farmland spread with fresh manure. Dirty public bathrooms, sticky restaurant tables, food service workers who wipe their noses...shall we go on?

Because we are human, these assaults on our senses of smell, touch, sight, hearing and taste—as well as our sense of dignity—are annoying, but fortunately, they are occasional rather than frequent.

I heard a story on the radio this morning about a couple, both blind and deaf, who raised three children, so I guess all is relative, and I really have little to complain about. But...do people really have to drive so damned slowly when I'm in a hurry to get to work? Or tailgate when I'm taking a leisurely drive?

Arrrrgh. (August 28, 2016)

Company's Coming!

Company's coming. That was the refrain in our household when I was young and my mother was preparing for overnight guests.

She'd scrub the floors, wash and iron curtains, make the beds with her best cotton sheets, and bring out the new towels she kept stored between tissue paper in dresser drawers. It was a big deal, having our relatives or friends come from afar. My mother threw open windows to air out rooms, cleaned rugs, polished furniture, vacuumed, and baked.

Oh, did she bake.

Blueberry and raspberry pies, cinnamon yeast rolls, strawberry shortcake with fresh cream, chocolate cake, molasses cookies, and her best homemade bread.

Anticipation was the name of the game. We were excited and eager for new faces and voices to fill up the house, rides to the ocean, shopping, and sitting around in the evenings catching up.

I think of my mother now as I prepare for company at our summer house on the lake. I find myself doing the same things she did, flying from room to room, scouring floors and bathrooms, polishing, primping and even sweeping cobwebs off the outside of the house.

Like Mom, I take out the best towels and sheets, air out rooms, make beds, and place welcoming gifts on dressers such as fresh flowers and candy.

The day that company is to arrive, I bake. Usually it's chocolate chip, oatmeal, or molasses cookies for our friends to snack on during their stay. I might make a cake, muffins, or my mother's homemade chocolate syrup to pour over ice cream.

Nick and Barbara come every summer from Massachusetts and Kimberly and Otis from New Hampshire. They typically arrive the third week of August, ready for adventure and always armed with food, wine, and gifts.

Barb and Nick bring special cheeses, crackers, jams, and a bagful of books Barb has read over the past year; Kim and Otis bring fresh corn on the cob from a farm stand along the way, plus homemade pesto or chowder.

We whip up a big meal the first night, report on what we've been doing since we last talked, hear updates on family, and make plans for the week.

We do a lot of laughing and telling stories, take day trips to the coast, sit by the lake, and enjoy sunsets. We'll swim, take boat rides, and reminisce.

We are fortunate to have known each other for nearly fifty years, Kim, Nick, and I. Barb and Otis entered the picture not long after.

Nick and I worked at our college newspaper together in Connecticut in the seventies. Kim, who attended a nearby dance conservatory, lived down the hall from me. The three of us became best friends. We've stayed in touch all these years through visits (some years more than others) and letters, Christmas cards, and phone calls.

We've been there for each other through thick and thin — marriages, divorces, illnesses, the deaths of our parents. We show up at a moment's notice.

They're more like family than friends to me, and getting ready for their arrival is more fun than work as I anticipate seeing their smiling faces.

There's nothing so delightful as waking in the morning to laughter coming from downstairs as the early risers brew coffee and hatch plans for the day. Yes, company's coming, and I'm counting down the days.

Ah, these sweet August days. (August 13, 2021)

Return to Baby Showers

I hadn't been to a baby shower in years.

The last one I attended several years ago was so over the top I remember praying I'd not be invited to another in a very long time. The gifts were numerous—as in a mountain of presents, some gigantic in size, that took the poor pregnant woman hours to unwrap as we women watched the clock and yawned. Mothers, aunts, grandmothers, cousins, and multiple friends oohed and aahed over all the baby paraphernalia, much of which I hadn't a clue about. By the time the party was over, the guest of honor looked as if she might give birth right then and there.

But the shower I attended in February was sweet, with just a handful of women in addition to the mother- and father-to-be. The hostess provided a nice lunch and surprised us with a couple of games, one where we were asked to count the number of chocolate candy kisses in a jar and the person who came closest won the jar. I guessed 108; the winner got it right at 116. We were each given a ticket with a number when we walked through the door. The hostess drew the number five, and I won a gift bag containing body lotion, perfume, and hand sanitizer from Bath & Body Works.

The baby gifts, many of which were pink because the mother is having a girl, were practical and colorful—a high chair, crib, lots of clothes, blankets, and other baby things. Then, a pretty cake was served.

It's funny how events like that can take you back. I remembered attending a baby shower with my mother when I was about ten, and all the women and girls were seated in a circle while the mom-to-be was perched in a big chair decorated with crepe paper. My grandmother and two great aunts were there, dressed impeccably in their nicest clothes, and we were served punch, petits fours, finger sandwiches, and fudge. Everyone was polite and respectful. The gifts were mostly baby outfits and cloth diapers, blankets, booties, bottles, and hand-knit sweaters. In those days, no one knew whether the mother was having a girl or a boy, so many of the gifts were white, yellow, gray, or green.

I was all eyes, soaking in every detail, from the design on the wallpaper to the chatter about babies—burping and bathing, teething and tantrums. It was all very grown up and foreign to me, the youngest of seven children who was naive about such things. I remarked to my sister at the recent baby shower that we are as old now as our great aunts were then, and did the young women sitting next to us regard us as that ancient? Were we dressed like old ladies?

One of the refreshing things about being around young parents-to-be is seeing their sense of hope and anticipation for the future. Their whole lives are ahead of them, and oh, the lessons they will learn, the heartbreaks they no doubt will encounter, the joy they will feel.

One doesn't want to warn them of what may be in store, good or bad. Life will take care of that, and experience. And then they will find themselves the elders in the room, smiling, nodding, and offering encouragement without judgment.

When it rains, it pours. A mere week after the recent baby shower, I'll be attending another, this time for a young woman who's having a boy. I expect there'll be a lot of blue floating about, but it won't be the figurative kind. With all the darkness assaulting our world, the promise of new life portends light, love, and laughter. A good reminder that really, all we have is each other.

And that's all that really matters. (February 18, 2019)

It's Later Than You Think

My husband will typically advise young people to enjoy their lives by warning, "It's later than you think."

It's true that life is short, although we don't think in those terms when we are young. When we were released from school for the summer, the long, carefree days stretched forever before us. Now they are over in the blink of an eye, and before we know it, it is Labor

Day. Why it is, I do not know exactly, but the phenomenon proves true: each year of our lives goes by faster than the last.

Click, click, click.

It is only when we start to creep toward retirement age that we begin to realize life doesn't go on forever—if, that is, we are lucky enough to have made it that far. Many are not so fortunate. We start to notice our legs aren't as limber, our fingers not as nimble, we tire more easily, and where once we were able to shop or hike or socialize all day and into the evening, we now are ready to hit the sack at 9 p.m.

Also, our minds aren't quite as sharp. We know the answer to a question on Jeopardy!, for instance, but the words won't come. We can visualize a place, but it takes us twice the amount of time to utter its name. People tell me not to worry if I forget where I put my car keys—that happens to all of us now and then. But if we forget what keys are used for, then we've got something to worry about.

These things become more abundantly clear as we ease our way into summer, the time when we attend gatherings and parties and family reunions. We recently returned from a family reunion in Massachusetts for my husband's mother's side of the family. Only about a dozen of us attended, and we did a lot of laughing. When we returned to Maine with two of Phil's cousins and the spouse of one, we laughed some more. And then we watched old family films.

There they all were, tossing baseballs, playing in the lake, hula-hooping, wrestling with the dog, and waving to the camera as they pranced at Christmas into the houses of their aunts and uncles, all gone now. We watched with a mix of amusement and nostalgia: amusement for the goofy way kids acted for the camera and nostalgia for the past.

Yes, the time is ticking down. Our lives are two-thirds to three-quarters gone. We've spent years running and rushing around in a sea of people. In the race to get ahead, we find ourselves standing still. But that is, after all, life, isn't it?

As we dive into this summer of 2019, we know we can't slow down time. But we may at least create that illusion by stopping to smell the flowers and reminding ourselves that it is later than we think.

And by counting our blessings. Yes, every one. (June 17, 2019)

Closing up Camp

I ride my old L.L.Bean bike down the bumpy camp road to the main highway, three times up and three times back.

It is cool these mid-September mornings, refreshing, unlike pedaling in July or August when a more preferable exercise is to jump off the dock into the lake. But now that summer is waning and we are packing up, I tend to do all the things I don't take the time to do in the rush of summer, like riding my bike and hanging out on the dock to watch the loons paddle by when there are no boats on the water.

In the chilly mornings, I take the old rocking chair from the garage, set it just inside the overhead door where the sun beats in but there's no wind, and open my book. There's no rushing, and when I look up from a page, all I see are green trees and lawn. The last two weeks at camp, we slowly pack up the things we know we won't need—hot weather clothes, food from the fridge and cupboards, cleaning fluids we know will freeze over the winter, a radio, magazines, books, a food processor I ferry between home and camp each year.

It is a sad process, having to close up camp, but as the nights get cold, we know it is time to go. Even the cats know, instinctively. They seem restless and look us in the eye as if to ask, "When?"

Our camp on China Lake.

This has been a cold second week of September in Maine. The thing I love most about camp is that all summer long, we can leave windows open, day and night, feel the air blow through, hear the wind and rain and especially the call of the loons. But with the windows and bedroom doors closed up tight to conserve heat, it is particularly quiet. We turn on the little electric heater with a fake flame, don flannel shirts and thick socks, and cozy up on the living room sofas.

We have already hauled the lawn furniture into the garage, ripped up cucumber and tomato plants from the garden, taken hanging flowers and potted herbs home, and removed solar lights from either side of the front steps. The guest rooms are packed up, towels and linens washed, folded, and put away, and beds covered. Kitchen cupboards and fridge are nearly bare, containing only a few days' necessities.

It is hard to go, but prolonging departure is torturous. It does not help that the weather turns cold and then hot again, first urging us to go, then coaxing us to stay. At some point, I realize it is not just leaving that makes me sad but having to say goodbye to summer, too, and all that it represents—warmth, carefree days, visitors, forays to the coast, the occasional ice cream cone.

But once we go, I also know there will be new things to do—the house to spiff up, gardens to weed and clear out, fall plans to make. Though I tend to forget from year to year, once we are settled in and the cats reacclimated, there always comes a day, not long after arriving, that I declare the inevitable.

"It's good to be home." (September 16, 2019)

Maine's Odd, Quirky Road Names

Didn't my new coworker laugh when she was writing the cop log one day and came across a street in Freedom, Maine called Goosepecker Ridge.

Molly Shelly, who landed here from Pennsylvania three months ago, has since been learning all sorts of things about central Maine and the state in general. She loves it here. More recently, she discovered Grumpy Men Avenue in Anson—you can't make this stuff up—and doubled over in laughter.

"In Anson, Friday at 10:32 a.m., a theft was reported on Grumpy Men Avenue," the log says.

It's true, we Mainers have a propensity for dreaming up crazy, quirky, and peculiar street and road names. I told Molly she hadn't yet come across Sesame, Big Bird, Boo, and Blah streets in Skowhegan. Or Chicken Street in the town of Starks.

And, of course, there's Katie Crotch Road in Embden where the road sign has been stolen many, many times, according to eighty-nine-year-old Eleanor Ketchum, the town's E911 addressing officer. Ketchum told me a family with the last name "Cadie" lived on a corner of the road a very long time ago, and over the years, the name got twisted.

"That's people for you," Ketchum said. "Just like other things, one person mispronounces something just a little, and next thing you know, somebody picked that up, and away it goes."

Somerset County has some of the most unusual names: Hole in the Wall Road in Athens; No Way, also in Athens; Shy Road in Palmyra; Rowdy Lane and Weed Lane in Burnham—do they smoke something there?—and Notta Road in Canaan. Newport, in Penobscot County, has a Down Wind Boulevard. I wonder what it's down-wind of?

One street name that particularly caught my eye: Bactasanity Drive in Moscow, which is way up north near Jackman. Madison, which has a Crazy Lane, must be in competition. In Kennebec County, there's Bumpy Road, Piggery Road, Stephen King Drive (there's a plug for the Bangor horror writer), and White Rice Lane, all in Augusta. The town of Greene has Welcome Hill Road, in contrast to Goah Way, That Way, and This Way in Liberty.

There's a Dirt Road in Albion and an Opportunity Way in Waterville, and in Oakland, a Godown Trail and Electric Avenue. And similarly, Embden has a Kilowatt Drive. Gardiner is home to Dazzle Lane and Justa Way, Sidney boasts Mellow Hill, and the town of Fayette has Our Road. Thorndike, in Waldo County, has an eerie name—Coffin Road. I don't think I'd want to live there.

There are some other places I'd avoid, including Harm's Way in Belgrade, Dismal Drive in Monmouth, and Dyer Straits in Palermo. I hope there are detours around Hostile Valley Road in Palermo and Vipah Lane in Farmington. I wonder what neighbors do on that latter street, anyway? Palermo also has a Boots and Saddle Road (now there's a mouthful), and Fairfield's got a Skat Street. Skat of what?

There are some odd ones in Franklin County, including Hernia Hill Road in Carrabassett Valley (is that because ascending it results in injury?), Rough Drive in Strong, Tilt of the Kilt Road in Rangeley, and Crash Road in Jay.

Though central Maine communities certainly seem to employ the creative spark when it comes to naming streets, I've decided Skowhegan takes the grand prize for frequency. In addition to having Sesame, Big Bird, Boo, and Blah streets, Skowhegan also is home to MRI Drive, White Chicken Road, and Lois Lane. And to think I grew up there. Truly, a town after my own heart.

(September 30, 2019)

Where Does the Stamp Go?

"Do you have a postage stamp?"

Molly, my twenty-three-year-old colleague who sits next to me in the newsroom, asked the question.

"Sure."

I reached into my bag, plucked a stamp out of my pocket calendar, and handed it to her. A few seconds later, she posed another question.

"Um, where do you put it on the envelope?"

"The stamp?" I said. "Upper right-hand corner."

Before I had a chance to ask if she was serious, Molly said, "Do I fold this?"

She was holding up a copy of the W-2 form she planned to mail to her father.

I took the paper, folded the bottom up to the center of the page, folded the top down over it, and handed it back to her.

"Thanks," she said.

I asked Molly if they taught her in school how to address, stamp, and mail a letter.

"This is the first letter I've ever mailed," she said.

"Really? What if you want to send a birthday card to someone?"

"I hand it to them," she said, matter of factly.

Molly is a bright young woman with a degree from Temple University, who has interned at the Philadelphia Inquirer as well as the radio station NBC Sports Philadelphia. She is no slouch.

I opened my mouth to respond but instead asked my editor, who is older than I am, if he was hearing this conversation.

"Yes," he said, without turning from his computer.

I pressed Molly. Did they teach her cursive writing in school? Oh, yes, she effused. Did she learn how to fill out a check? No.

"I wrote a check for the first time this year—to pay my rent," she said.

Two things crossed my mind. I'm old, at sixty-three. And I might be in the twilight zone.

I turned to another colleague Taylor Abbott, who is twenty-two.

"Taylor, do you know how to send a letter?"

"Of course," she said. "My parents taught me how to do that a long time ago. I know how to write a check, too."

Taylor said she also has sent packages but only through Amazon. In other words, she has ordered gifts online, paid an extra five dollars to have them wrapped, and never actually touched the gift or package itself.

"But I would have trouble sending packages at the post office," she said. "I would need some help."

I thought at this point about all the letters, cards, and packages I've mailed over my lifetime. I couldn't imagine not knowing how to do that. There are so many things I've experienced over the last few years that make me realize time is moving on and so am I, but this dialogue with my younger colleagues tops them all.

Don't get me wrong. I love working with them. They are constantly teaching me things about technology that are foreign to me but second nature to them. They grew up with it, after all. Kind of like my knack for mailing letters.

After some deliberation, I've decided this symbiotic relationship really is fortuitous; I've got institutional memory and experience that Molly and Taylor draw on, and they bring a whole new perspective and set of skills to the newsroom.

In that vein, I am reminded of a sign I saw years ago outside a small gas station and store in western Maine: "If you don't stop, we're both gonna starve."

Yep. We both reap the benefits. (March 13, 2020)

Wicked Puzzling Maine Terms

Phil's relatives stared at him blankly when he declared we've been on screech these last few weeks.

"On screech?" Barry said. "What's that?"

Barry and Vivian Bergquist, who hail from Minnesota, and Barbara Gooch, from Georgia, said they had never heard the expression.

"It means you're doing too much and you are stressed," my husband explained.

I say "I'm on screech" so often that I was surprised our guests were unfamiliar with it.

I googled "on screech."

Although there was no definition for that expression as such, Merriam-Webster defines screech as a high, shrill piercing cry, usually expressing pain or terror. It also can mean howl, scream, shriek, shrill, squall, squeal, yell, or yelp. A slang definition offered online for screech as a verb: to act excessively, especially while on marijuana.

Not exactly what I was looking for, but interesting nonetheless.

Could "on screech" be an expression exclusive to Maine? Our discussion last week reminded me of a conversation I had recently with a new neighbor who moved here from Washington state.

Earlier in the summer, I had told her we were going to our place on China Lake. A few weeks later, she approached me and asked if we had been at our "camp," though she uttered the word with what I sensed was a bit of hesitation as if she were not sure she had used the right term. She explained she had never heard "camp" used to describe such a place. When people told her they were going up to camp, she envisioned a tent, or encampment of tents, like where drifters might congregate.

Phil's cousins Barry and Vivian said that in Minnesota, people refer to what we call camps as cabins or, less frequently, cottages. Our friend Irv Rosenberg, formerly of Harpswell and now living in California, calls them cottages, as do characters on the fifties television show Perry Mason, set and filmed in California.

Which gets me to thinking about other terms we Mainers use that may sound strange to those living elsewhere.

As kids, we referred to the activity of descending the stairs into the basement of our house as "going down cellar."

In elementary school, my friend Juline would report she was heading to the restroom by saying she was "going to the basement."

Not sure how that term came to be, but now that I think of it, other kids called it the basement, too.

Phil remembers rural Mainers years ago using "whan't" instead of "wasn't" or "weren't," as in "Whan't that funny?"

Folks also referred to someone as "numb," as opposed to "dumb."

My maternal grandmother would exclaim, "I shan't go there today," rather than " I shall not."

She also, when talking on the telephone, would respond, "Ayuh, ayuh, ayuh," to the person on the other end of the line. Wouldn't it have been easier to just say, "Yup, yup, yup"?

In the sixties, my friend Patty, on a hot summer day, would declare it was time to go buy a "sody" or a "sody pop." That's an expression you don't hear much anymore.

Boys in the neighborhood referred to puttering and performing menial chores as "dubbin' around."

Sometimes we didn't even use words to communicate. Like when a car passed by, instead of waving, we'd just tilt our heads backward.

This is all to say, I guess, that we Mainers had, and still have, a unique and inimitable way of being in the world. Which is wicked good for us. We wouldn't want to claim being from anywhere else. Like, from away. (August 5, 2022)

The "New Normal"

Bitsy pops up on the chair beside me and butts her furry head against my arm as if to say, "What's going on here?" It's Wednesday, Day 3 of my working from home because of the coronavirus pandemic, and the dining room table has become my new office. It's littered with papers, notebooks, double computer screens, a keyboard, and a phone. My portable police scanner, plugged into the outlet around the corner, squawks on and off. Bitsy, our gray and black cat, has known me long enough to figure anything is possible here, so she's not too upset. But still, she looks questioningly.

This is our new normal.

It's the first time in more than thirty years that I've worked from home, a mile away from my newspaper office in Waterville. I'm not flying out the door every day and returning, hours later.

It is nine in the morning, and the aroma of beans baking in the oven all day wafts through my work space. In the next room, Perry Mason, the fictional attorney from decades ago, is arguing a court case on the television show of the same name. My husband keeps the volume low as he tries to accommodate my needs.

"It doesn't bother me, really" I tell him. "I can barely hear it."

I wonder how Phil is faring in this new world of ours. He has always said he wishes I'd retire, but I'm not ready for that.

"Be careful what you wish for," I told him.

Two days into my working from home, he informed me that I'm too aggressive on the keyboard.

"You know, you hit those keys pretty hard. You're going to break them. Every time you get an idea, it's bang, bang—bang, bang, bang."

I remind him I've always typed this way. It comes from having learned on an old Royal typewriter when I was ten.

I've decided there are silver linings in this new routine, although I do miss my colleagues and the din of their voices discussing stories in the newsroom. I went for a walk yesterday and today, something I don't do enough of in my normal life. I've decided to do it every day to relieve stress during these uncertain times. That's what the experts say—fresh air is good for us and doesn't carry the coronavirus.

Nary a car passed me on my half-hour walk yesterday. I could hear birds chirping loudly from a faraway tree. I might have imagined it, but the atmosphere smelled cleaner, with fewer vehicles on the roads and planes in the air. Today, several people were out walking.

"It's nice to see a human being, even though we have to stand twenty feet apart," I said to a woman pushing a stroller.

I passed the North Street Playground, where a small family was recreating. A Waterville school van was parked there with its back door open, ready to hand out food to kids. I waved to the driver. A neighborhood friend was outside her house. We chatted briefly. She wondered aloud how long this will go on.

"They're saying it could be eighteen months until they have a vaccine," she said.

These days, I am reminded of my childhood, when most of our entertainment was what we initiated ourselves—climbing trees, building cabins in the woods, swimming, skiing, and reading books. Television was a relatively new thing, and we only got a couple of channels, so we didn't watch it much.

I can't help but think that, as tough as this new normal is, it is an opportunity for us to go back to that simpler existence. To prove to ourselves that we are capable of functioning without running here and there, buying products we probably don't need, always grasping for something. It is a meditative time, as I see it—a chance to sit back, breathe, and think about what's really important.

Day three has already shown me that with time, the fear does lessen as we adjust to our new routines, heed precautions, and carry on.

(March 20, 2020)

Cats are Perfect Pandemic Partners

It's awfully nice to have cats around during the holiday season.

That's not to say they aren't good companions all year long, but during the winter—and in this pandemic—they are especially good company. The minute I started wrapping gifts, they were right there, fascinated with every ribbon I cut and curled, every paper I sliced, every note written.

Thurston is a large, three-year-old, orange and white cat; Bitsy is fourteen years old and a gray, white, and black tiger. Thurston likes to pounce on her sometimes. She gets annoyed. For the most part, they get along fine, particularly when they go outdoors where they are comrades against the fierce world.

Cats have their curiosities, which we haven't quite figured out. We suspect they know more than they let on. For instance, how does one explain the following phenomenon?

Whenever I go to the refrigerator and pluck out two little containers of yogurt and remove spoons from the drawer, Thurston is at my feet before I can get to the living room to hand one to Phil. Thurston can be sleeping deeply in another room but never fails to appear when yogurt is being fetched. Remove ice cream from the freezer or seltzer from the fridge, and he doesn't budge. But that yogurt.

Full disclosure: we always allow the cats to have a lick of the yogurt container after we've emptied them. That likely serves as an incentive. But we have tried retrieving yogurt several different ways and at different times of the day just to test Thurston. I tiptoe to the kitchen and open the silverware drawer without a sound, and still, he appears out of nowhere.

Bitsy is old enough to know the drill when the Christmas tree comes into the house, and she is not fazed. Thurston, on the other hand, flees to another room when he deems a marauder has entered his

Thurston and Bitsy.

quiet domain. Bitsy watches intently as we set up the tree and I decorate; Thurston stands at a distance. With time, he acclimates, and they take naps under the tree. No matter how fresh the water is in their bowls, they drink water out of the tree stand all season long.

The cats love to frolic in the snow and sun themselves on the deck, but they are not fond of rain. When they come in after an active day, Bitsy heads to the guest room where she snoozes on the bed by the window. Thurston goes to Phil's closet in the bedroom, curls up in a dark corner on the floor, and sleeps for hours. The house becomes strangely quiet.

By early evening, Bitsy will appear, and, just as Jeopardy! starts, Thurston rounds the corner of the hallway. Bitsy curls up on a red throw beside Phil on the short sofa. Thurston leaps onto the long couch where I sit, nuzzles into the blue afghan my mother knit years ago, and purrs. Is there any better sound than that of a purring cat?

I don't know what pet-less people do, especially during a pandemic. I can't imagine being without ours. I'm sure dog owners feel the same. The irony is that they rely on us for everything, yet we're the ones who reap the benefits. The way I see it, there's no more purr-fect partners than cats during this pandemic holiday season.

Or at any other time, for that matter. (December 11, 2020)

Discovering What Really Matters

I never thought I'd see the day when the prospect of taking a drive to Portland would generate excitement. But that has come to pass, thanks to the coronavirus pandemic.

One of the things it has taught us is how precious are the simple things we take for granted. This thought came to me when I asked my sister if she had a good birthday. She traveled to Portland, got takeout food, and splurged at a kitchen store using a gift card she'd received. What an exciting foray, I thought, admittedly with a sense of longing to do the same.

It has been nearly a year since we have eaten in a restaurant, taken a long drive to another town or state, patronized the theater or symphony, stayed overnight in a hotel, or shopped just for the heck of it.

The upside, I suppose, is that my checkbook balance is plumper, there's less wear and tear on my vehicle, and I fill the gas tank less often.

My birthday in March will be the second during which I will not have celebrated with family and friends because of the pandemic—and I am always one to love a birthday party. We did host an outdoor, socially distanced, and masked birthday gathering for my sister in our snowy backyard last weekend, attended by my two other sisters, one of whom baked a delicious cheesecake topped with strawberries. There was the opening of gifts, sipping of hot drinks, and lively banter during the hour-long visit. We laughed at how bizarre it was to celebrate a birthday while bundled up in winter attire, including ski pants.

Imagine what it will be like to gather as we used to do, without fear of getting sick. How will any of us who lived through the pandemic not recognize how fortunate that is?

I remember my parents and grandmothers recounting all the things people couldn't do, eat, buy, or see during the Great Depression. Many lost jobs and were poor. As a result, they rarely threw anything away because they might need it one day—a practice we baby boomers found amusing. But our elders operated with caution because they endured tough times. They remembered the past. So too will we, I think, once we emerge from the pandemic.

One day, we'll look back on this strange time, when we hurried through the grocery store, masked and hoping not to see anyone we knew so we wouldn't have to stop and chat. We'll remember what it was like spending most of our time at home. That will have included being relegated to working at home—at least for those of us lucky enough to have kept our jobs.

We became acclimated to our homes and found comfort in activities like being able to throw a meal in the oven and go back to work or take a brief walk outside. We didn't travel a lot, and a trip to the ocean was a treat. We shopped when we needed something—we didn't do it just for fun. Instead of buying more stuff, we took care of what we had. Going to the movies or drive-in was an infrequent and, thus, thrilling occurrence. We created our own excitement, year-round. We scoured the woods and fields in summer and skied, tobogganed, and skated in winter. When the weather was bad, we stayed in and read books.

Living in this pandemic reminds me frequently of William Wordsworth's sonnet "The World is Too Much With Us," published in 1807 and often cited aloud by my late father:

> The world is too much with us; late and soon,
> Getting and spending, we lay waste our powers;
> Little we see in Nature that is ours;
> We have given our hearts away, a sordid boon!

More than two hundred years later, Wordsworth's words still ring true. As horrid as this pandemic is, it has taught us about what really matters. (January 22, 2021)

THE PEOPLE I MEET

Waving Goodbye to a Friend

It's a truism that you don't always know the impact a person makes on the world until they die. Often, it only becomes evident by the number of people who show up for a funeral or the sympathy cards that pile up after someone you love passes away. You might say Don Hennessy's legacy to Waterville was evident by the crowd that took to the streets Sunday, waving at motorists and smiling just like Hennessy did for so many years. Known throughout the city as "the Waver," Hennessy died last week at seventy-six.

Until a year ago, he walked the streets of the city nearly every day, dressed in black and waving, using hand and arm movements that actually were martial arts blocking techniques. During winter, he often donned a black knitted mask that covered everything but his eyes and mouth, sometimes prompting an out-of-towner to call the police claiming they saw a bank robber on the loose. But Hennessy was anything but a menace. He was humble and kind—and well loved even by many people who didn't know him.

I accompanied Hennessy on a walk just before Christmas in 2009. He was living in a Main Street apartment, nearly blind and suffering from osteoarthritis of the spine. He hurt all over.

"I don't have a spot in my body that doesn't," he said. "I have to walk. I've got no choice. If I didn't do it, I'd be in bed for the rest of my life."

Hennessy told me he had eleven disabilities, including macular degeneration, which prevented him from watching the many Clint Eastwood movies stacked neatly in a box at his feet.

"I have a difficult time with it," he says. "If it wasn't for the fact that I know what I'm doing and where I am, I wouldn't be able to be on my own."

Born in Portland during the thirties, he was sickly as a child and suffered from tuberculosis empyema. He never went to school. "I don't have a formal education. I've had to learn everything the hard way. I can't read, and I can't write."

When he got older, in the fifties and sixties, he worked in his brother-in-law's catering business, driving a truck and delivering food. He married four times, but his wives all left him, he said.

When he moved to Waterville several years ago, he helped landlords with raking and other chores, but eventually, his physical troubles interfered. He says he sometimes goes into a cataleptic state where his muscles become rigid and he cannot move.

In his second-floor apartment the day I visited, Hennessy sat in a recliner, his white hair, mustache, and long sideburns framing green eyes that do not focus on any particular thing. He apologized frequently for not being able to remember certain things or articulate what he wanted to say.

The sparsely furnished apartment was small and dark, with a living room and kitchen separated by an archway. The rooms were meticulously neat. Beside Hennessy's recliner was a small wooden table that housed pencils, a telephone, and other items lined up carefully just within reach.

His shelves featured statues of Samurai warriors and Buddhas. Swords, knives, and other weapons hung on the walls among large velvet paintings of tigers and lions. Hennessy said he was heavily involved in martial arts earlier in his life.

Despite all his ailments, walking helped—that is, until about a year ago, when he couldn't do it any longer, according to his best friend, Jimmy Buck of Fairfield.

Buck, now fifty-six, had known Hennessy for forty-one years. Hennessy took Buck under his wing during Buck's difficult teenage years and became like a father to him. Years later, Buck became Hennessy's caretaker. He'd pick him up at his apartment and drive him to his home in Fairfield for Christmas with his family, and, when Hennessy could no longer cook, he ferried meals to his apartment. Last November, Hennessy moved to an assisted-living facility, and that's where he died on May 18, 2011, with Buck by his side. Like his life, death was not easy.

"He had the death rattle," Buck said. "He got pneumonia. He was gasping for air. It was a blessing when he went."

But Hennessy died knowing he was somewhat of a local celebrity. Buck said he enjoyed being recognized as the Waver.

"He loved it. He lived for that. That was just his whole life. I mean, he was all alone, and that was great attention for him."

So Hennessy would likely be delighted to know that about forty-five people walked Sunday from Hannaford at Elm Plaza, where he shopped for food, to the public library, waving to people and smiling in his honor.

Someone also set up a Facebook page in his memory, with people from all over saying complimentary things about him.

"It was always nice to see your friendly wave as I drove by the city of Waterville. You'll be missed. May you rest with the angels now and be at peace. The city of Waterville has lost one of a kind, but they sure will remember you forever," said Melissa Pierce.

Buck said he saw a picture of the walk and didn't recognize one person in it, so Hennessy must have had many admirers.

"Apparently, he touched them somehow."

The Waver will be cremated and his ashes buried in a private and simple ceremony soon at the Maine Veterans Memorial Cemetery in Augusta, Buck said.

He won't be alone. We'll all be there in spirit, waving our last goodbye. (May 28, 2011)

The "Cross Man"

John Lewis was laid to rest Friday in a peaceful cemetery off Grove Street, just inches from the mother he loved dearly.

Lewis, sixty-nine, was known to us Watervillians as the Cross Man, because we'd see him every day about town, waving his cross and blessing everyone and everything in his path. He once told me he spreads love because there's so much hate in this country.

"People should love one another," he said.

Lewis told me this in 2007 when I walked a few miles with him in the dead of winter, snow pelting us in the face and a cold wind blowing against our backs. I was chilled to the bone, but Lewis wasn't. He marched through the streets day and night, summer and winter, through all kinds of weather. It was his mission to spread love, he said, and he had a lot of it to give. So when he died in his bed on a Tuesday in 2012, in his meticulously neat apartment on Western Avenue, I figured his work must have been done.

"He passed in his sleep, the way he wanted it," said his friend Dan McNulty at his graveside.

McNulty, Lewis' friend of twenty-five years, and Steve Nadeau, funeral director of Veilleux Funeral Home, led the short, simple service.

John Lewis on the streets of Waterville. Photo by David Leaming | *Morning Sentinel*.

"He loved life, and he looked to share the gospel of Jesus Christ with all who would listen," McNulty said.

Lewis, he said, is now at peace.

"We can rejoice knowing John is where he wanted to be—at the foot of Jesus Christ, our lord and savior."

About sixty people turned out for the service, arriving in cars, on foot, and even on bicycles. Sister Kathryn Kelm, affectionately known as Sister Kay Kay, pedaled her bicycle on the dirt roads that meander through St. Francis Cemetery, parked it, and met everyone with a smile.

It was a hot and humid day. At first, it was quiet, with only McNulty and his wife, Denise; Nadeau; Lewis' sister, Marie Menendez of Pittsfield; and his brother, Robert Lewis of Connecticut, standing by the grave. Mike Hebert, facilities manager for Corpus Christi Parish, was also there.

Then more people came, seemingly out of nowhere and wearing street clothes. They gathered by the large white stone bearing the name Arthur Castonguay who, according to Hebert, was Lewis' grandfather. Castonguay was the first soldier from Waterville killed in combat during World War I and for whom Castonguay Square in downtown Waterville is named.

Lewis' plain wooden coffin, draped with lovely pink, red, and white flowers, lay before the stone.

Hebert told me later that Lewis would be buried just a couple of inches from his mother, a detail I found comforting. Lewis told me lots of personal stories when I met him in 2007 about how he was slow as a child, had a hard time in school, quit in the tenth grade, and had difficulty understanding things.

"My mother would try to help me figure things out," he said. "My mama was a beautiful soul. She was my life. She loved the Lord enormously. My mother was my star. She was something special. She said, 'Be good to people. If somebody needs a dollar, give it to them.'"

For ten years, he took care of his mother, who had become very ill, he said. He was overcome with fear that she would die, and when she finally did in 2002 at eighty-one years old, Lewis was devastated.

"I've never got over it. I dream about her every night," he said. "She was good to me. At the end, I fell apart. I wouldn't let go of my mama."

At the time, Lewis was also mourning the death of his beloved parrot, Peppi, whose ashes he kept on a stool by his Christmas tree. The bird was his companion for forty-five years until it died in 2005. Lewis loved deeply, and he loved well. He even loved those who threw rocks at him and taunted him as he walked the streets.

At his service Friday, twenty-two-year-old Catherine Sands of Clinton said she watched him wave his cross all her life. She met him when she was a small child, and the first thing he said to her was "bless you."

"You could be the most awful person in the world, and he would still bless you. He was an angel, here on earth," she said.

Becky Emery, sixty-two, of Waterville, remembered working with Lewis some thirty years ago at the former Cascade Woolen Mill in Oakland. When she became very sick once, he walked miles to visit her.

"He walked all the way down in a snowstorm and brought me flowers and chocolates, and I had my brother drive him home," she said.

After I wrote a story about Lewis a few days before Christmas in 2007, he visited me at the newspaper and brought me a Christmas card. And for every Christmas thereafter, like clockwork, he'd deliver another. He was a kind, generous, and loving man, one who will not soon be forgotten.

Godspeed, my friend, John. And bless you. (July 7, 2012)

Peter Joseph and the Waterville Mills

Peter Joseph was eight in 1931 and he was learning the meaning of hard work in the family store, Joseph's Market, on Front Street in Waterville. He'd come in at six in the morning and sell cigarettes, chewing tobacco, and other items to millworkers, and then at eight, he'd walk across town to North Grammar School on Pleasant Street.

When school let out in the afternoon, he'd head back to the store and work some more.

"I remember every Friday, my mother made a Lebanese dish with lentils and black olives, and when I came home at lunchtime, I'd take the pot of food to Wyandotte Worsted woolen mill at Head of Falls where my father worked. I'd sit there while he ate his lunch, bring the pot back to my mother at the house, and then go back to school."

Joseph, who will be eighty-nine in October, recalled that his father, John R. Joseph Sr., did not want to leave the four looms that he ran in the mill, so he ate his lunch there.

"They were dedicated to their work, the people who worked in mills. He'd work there from seven o'clock in the morning until three in the afternoon and then go to work in the store."

Back then, the Wyandotte was one of several mills in the Waterville area that employed hundreds of people from the city and surrounding communities including Winslow, Oakland, and Fairfield.

The Wyandotte was just north of the Two-Cent Bridge—named such because people coming into the city from Winslow would pay two cents to cross it. Waterville Ironworks was farther up Front Street, near an old entry to the street that runs under the railroad tracks. Hollingsworth & Whitney Co. produced paper on the Winslow side of the Kennebec River; the Cascade Woolen Mill in Oakland was also bustling.

Waterville was a booming city then. Head of Falls was home to Lebanese, French, and some Italian families. C.F. Hathaway Co. workers made shirts at the factory north of Appleton Street, and the Lockwood Duchess Cotton mill complex on Water Street was also in full swing. Cigarettes were ten cents a pack, and most millworkers couldn't afford this, so Joseph's sold them individual cigarettes for a penny. The Joseph family was generous to poor people and often gave them food.

"People working the mills were making $16 or $17 a week," Peter Joseph recalled.

His father had come to America from Lebanon in 1900 and married Lena Ferris, also from Lebanon. They had six children, all of whom worked at the store, which John Joseph opened around 1926. Peter, the youngest, is the only child still alive. He and his late wife, Patricia, had six children, who also worked at the store.

Kevin Joseph, his nephew, now owns the business, but Peter continues to help out.

"I take care of the produce department—I order the produce," he said.

While he officially retired from the grocery business in 1985, he continues to work as a deacon at the nearby St. Joseph Maronite Catholic Church and as a per diem chaplain at Maine General Medical Center's Thayer Campus. The World War II veteran is also chairman of the Waterville Safety Council, on which he has served forty-six years. It's no stretch to say that it's people like Peter Joseph who have helped make this country great.

Even though it's Labor Day and a day off for many people, Joseph stands by, waiting to help those in need.

"I like to keep busy," he says. "I don't mind working—it's either that or doing the crossword. I never turn the TV on until after supper, and I usually watch comedy shows unless a good movie comes on with Clark Gable or Tyrone Power." (September 3, 2012)

Along the Passagassawakeag

Peter Reny climbs the steep steps into the train, sits in his perch by the open window, and starts the locomotive. It rumbles and spits and rolls into a rhythmic hum, warming up for the two-mile trip along the Passagassawakeag River, which empties into the ocean in Belfast.

Reny, sixty-six, of North Vassalboro, has engineered this scenic trip on the Belfast & Moosehead Lake Railroad hundreds of times, but this will be his last, at least on this stretch of track. The city of Belfast plans to rip up the track and turn it into a walking trail, a move Reny finds disturbing.

"I feel sad about it—really sad because every time you pull up a piece of rail, it's never going to go back, and you've lost the potential of passenger service, loss of freight," Reny says.

He has cause to be disheartened, having done just about every railroad job imaginable since he started working for railroads in 1966. He also was president of the Brotherhood of Railway Carmen for many years.

"Today is my anniversary with the railroad, forty-seven years," he says. "I was nineteen years old when I started, and I had to have a note from my mother to go to work. I started as a laborer for Maine Central Railroad off College Avenue in Waterville. I cut up boxcars for the stores department—the purchasing department."

Reny, wearing a blue and white striped engineer's cap, keeps his hands on the throttle and brakes and, when he crosses a road or bridge, sounds the bell and blasts the whistle. This locomotive is pulling three coaches, an open-air car, and a caboose over the old tracks as it carries about one hundred passengers on its last trip along this shore.

The open-air car next to the locomotive is packed with people of all ages standing at the rail or sitting on benches, taking photos and soaking in the striking orange and red fall foliage on this bright

October Sunday afternoon. Sea gulls skim the salt water in the distance, where houses are perched on rocks beneath a blue and sunny sky.

"This is the best part of the whole trip, right here," Reny says. "It is the thing people love to see."

We crawl along at between five and fifteen miles per hour in the cab of the old locomotive, whose conductor this day is Thor Swenson, thirty-nine, also of Vassalboro. Reny explains that it is a diesel electric locomotive, built the same month and year he was born—November 1946.

Reny grew up in North Vassalboro, the seventh of eight children. He was drawn to all things mechanical and started working on cars at a young age. Today, he has sixty classic and antique cars, trucks, and tractors that he shows at various events and volunteers to take to nursing homes for people to enjoy.

"I was probably just starting school, and my father had me taking things apart, like farm tractors," he says. "My father was a farmer, and he also worked in a textile mill—the American Woolen Mill [in Vassalboro]."

Pete Reny's first car was a 1933 Plymouth—like the one in the film *American Graffiti*.

"I was fifteen. I started collecting cars at seventeen—I had a Model A Ford. It drove my father crazy. He was neat as a pin. My mother had to stick up for me. She said, 'At least he's not running the streets—we know where he is.'"

Reny knows cars well and is known around the state by auto aficionados. He and his wife, Jackie, have many friends who stop at his busy Route 32 shop to check out his collection and latest acquisitions. They also like to hear his train stories and hear all about the colorful characters he worked with as he moved up the ladder in the railroad, from laborer to car repairman, welder, air brakeman, car inspector, engineer, and supervisor.

151

Belfast & Moosehead Lake Railroad train engineer Peter Reny. Photo by Amy Calder.

Reny worked mostly for Maine Central Railroad but also for the Bangor & Aroostook and St. Lawrence & Atlantic railroads. He retired in 2007 but continues to volunteer as an engineer on the Belfast & Moosehead. In addition to the scenic rides, he also takes passengers to and from the annual Common Ground Fair, an event hosted in Unity each fall by the Maine Organic Farmers and Gardeners Association. The Belfast train, he said, was owned by Maine Central Railroad in the 1800s when it hauled freight, passengers, and mail.

"I came here as an engineer in 1989 and hauled freight—mostly wood, oil pearlite, and some coal."

As we amble along the tracks on this last trip to the ocean, the car wheels squealing and scraping against the rail, Reny is uncharacteristically quiet. I know he is committing every rock, tree, hill, and turn to memory. We enter the station at City Point, and he rings the bell and blasts the whistle as he always does.

But this time, I detect a tear in his eye. (October 20, 2013)

A Four-Legged Friend

Wilbur is not the most beautiful dog in the world. He has a crooked face and is broad across the chest, which makes him look bow-legged. Beyond that, the thirteen-year-old, black-and-white, beagle-bull terrier mix is slowing down a bit, and his brown eyes are getting cloudy.

"The parts don't fit together very well," his owner, Cindy Longstaff, acknowledges. "See, he's got a snaggle-tooth, and sometimes his lip will get caught under his tooth, and he has this funny-looking grin."

While he may be considered kind of ugly, the children at Albert S. Hall School in Waterville think Wilbur is just lovely. A few times a week, Longstaff, seventy-five, walks Wilbur to the elementary school on Pleasant Street, where he greets the children getting off the school bus. They have been doing this for about four years.

The tradition started when Longstaff and Wilbur stopped on their walk one day to visit the school crossing guard. A small bus with special needs students pulled up to the curb to let children out, and there was a particular boy who did not look happy at all. Longstaff noticed that the next day, he seemed similarly morose.

"He was in a foul mood, and he was having a terrible time," Longstaff recalled. "Somewhere along the line, he started getting off the bus with a big grin when he saw Wilbur."

It was then that Longstaff decided she'd bring the dog regularly to the bus stop to greet the students.

"Everybody comes by and strokes his ears," she said. "Some are timid, but they kind of get over that. They learn that he's just there to say, 'Good morning,' and I think they relate to that."

On a cloudy, raw Wednesday last week, I accompanied Longstaff and Wilbur on their walk to school. At seven-thirty in the morning, we crossed Pleasant Street from the home Longstaff has shared for forty years with her husband, state Rep. Thomas R.W. Longstaff. Wilbur plodded along, sniffing the wet leaves and puddles on the sidewalks, his skinny tail wagging to and fro. We crossed to Nudd Street with Longstaff explaining how Wilbur came into their lives several years ago when his owner, a neighbor, moved away and left him in their care. Wilbur at the time was a nervous dog and leery of people.

"He's come a long way in socializing himself with people," Longstaff said. "When he first came to us, he'd spin—he'd just go round and round in a circle."

We continued to Dalton Street, which feeds out onto Pleasant. Frannie Brown, the crossing guard, was in front of the school, walking kids across the street.

"Hi, Wilbur," she called, reaching down to pat the canine. "This is our mascot."

Brown, also seventy-five, has been the crossing guard for thirty-six years. She and Cindy Longstaff met years ago when their children were both on school swim teams. Brown said Wilbur is so popular that he was featured prominently in the school's yearbook.

"The special needs bus is the one that gets the biggest kick out of Wilbur," she said.

The activity quickened on the street, as buses, cars, and parents with children converged at the bus stop. Brown escorted children across the street as other kids poured out of buses. Some stopped to pat Wilbur as Longstaff wished them a happy Thanksgiving.

"Hey, Wilbur," a boy carrying a cello said, bending to greet the dog. "I won't hurt you. I don't want Wilbur to be afraid of me, just because I have this big instrument."

He introduced himself as Kaleb Macomber, age ten. The fifth-grader said he has known Wilbur for two years, ever since he started at Albert Hall School, and likes him a lot.

"He's my favorite dog, because he's always here in the morning for us to say 'Hi' and pet him," Macomber said. "And it seems as if he's just a good dog."

Nat Minot, age ten, was one of the last students to arrive at school. He embraced Wilbur with both hands.

"I'm patting Wilbur two times at once," he said.

Early in November, Minot wrote a poem about Wilbur that says:

"Who can be angry?/ Who can be sad?/ With a cute little puppy around/ With floppy little ears/ A silly little face/ And a cute little nose so round/ You may try to ignore it/ But you can't help but

Cindy Longstaff and her dog Wilbur greet Albert S. Hall School student Nat Minot. Photo by David Leaming | *Morning Sentinel.*

adore it/ And pet it and scratch it and laugh/ Who can be angry?/ Who can be sad?/ With a cute little puppy around!"

As Minot climbed the school steps, Principal Barbara Jordan stepped out to say hello to Longstaff and Wilbur. Jordan said the dog is a welcoming presence at the school.

"Wilbur's special because he brings joy to the students when they get off the bus—joy and happiness," Jordan said. "It starts the day positively for many of the students. And for Cindy to come each day and make a special point to be here, it speaks volumes for who she is, her character. It's just another adult making a difference in the lives of children." (November 27, 2016)

Waterville's Top Bird

Crows really are fascinating creatures. After I wrote a column about a dead crow I found in my backyard, I received lots of interesting comments from people relating their own experiences with crows. However, none were more compelling than the story I heard from Nancy Foster of Waterville.

She said that in the early fifties, her cousins Joy and Lee Bureau had a pet crow named Smokey, and he was smart and mischievous and so well known about town that when he died, his obituary appeared on the front page of the *Morning Sentinel.*

"Smokey wreaked havoc with the police, as he was always stealing parking tickets off car windows in downtown Waterville," Foster wrote. "I remember that he would fly into Woolworth's and pick up a sparkly bracelet and fly away. Stores back then didn't have air conditioning—doors were commonly left open."

I had to know more about Smokey, so I called Lee Bureau, and we had a good long chat about the crow, who was a celebrity in Waterville.

Bureau's sister Joy befriended the crow, who had fallen out of a nest. At first, she kept it in a cage, where she fed it and talked to it every day and taught it to say "Hello," Bureau said. Smokey then learned other words, much to the amazement of everyone, and he recognized faces, particularly those of Bureau family members.

The family lived on North Street. Lee Bureau, who was fifteen at the time, slept outside in a tent all summer, he said. He had a newspaper route and had to get up at four-thirty, and Smokey would act as his alarm clock—flying into the tent every morning and pecking and pulling at his blanket. If that didn't work, the crow became more aggressive, said Bureau, now eighty.

"He'd jump right up on my head and take his beak and stick it in my ear, like there was something in there," Bureau recalled. "It was just a riot—four-thirty and he gets me up. I'd get on my motor scooter, and he'd ride on my shoulder. I'd go over the North Street bridge, and there was something about it he liked. He'd spread his wings and disappear, and I kept going. I'd see him off in the distance. He'd play games. When I'd slow down, he'd come back, and he'd be on my shoulder, and we'd be eye-to-eye, and he'd make funny noises. The bird was amazing. He knew my paper route better than I did."

While Smokey lived on the Bureau property, he also flew around town and especially liked Rummel's ice cream stand on Silver Street.

"People'd feed him. They didn't know what to make of him. He had quite a vocabulary. People just couldn't believe it. He flew all over the city. People would call up and say, 'Your bird's over here. He took clothespins off my line.'"

Sometimes, Smokey would remove clothesline catches, which caused people's sheets to drag on the ground, according to Bureau.

"He liked little things—eyeglasses, nickels, combs—shiny things. He had a secret place down by the high school, a three-story apartment house, in the eaves of the building. Everybody kept saying he's got his stuff up there, but nobody dared to go up."

Bureau's father, Harvey, finally got a forty-foot ladder that reached up to the spot, and they found the stash, he said.

Smokey loved raw hamburger, and when he got hungry, he'd fly home to get some. Bureau said the crow could see a hamburger from a long distance.

One day, the crow plucked two hundred dollars in cash from Bureau's father's T-shirt pocket as he was talking to the local football coach in the driveway and flew up to the chimney on the roof next door. Fearing Smokey would release the money from his beak and drop it into the chimney, they took action.

"My father said, 'Quick, Lee, go get some hamburg,' so I ran in the house and got some hamburg. Smokey saw the hamburg and dropped the money, and the money was rolling down the roof."

One of the most amazing things about Smokey is that he knew what classrooms Lee and his sister attended all day at the old high school—now Gilman Apartments on Gilman Street.

"He'd land on the window sill and peck on the glass," Bureau recalled. "He knew where my sister was. My French teacher was scared to death. I said, 'Don't be afraid. It's just my pet crow.' I went to the window, and he'd walk back and forth on the window sill outside and then fly off."

Bureau credits his sister Joy, who died many years ago, for spending so much time with Smokey that he became part of the family and could learn to talk. Smokey, who was Bureau's best buddy for about three years, ultimately met a sad end in 1952.

It was winter, and the crow lived in the garage when it was cold, but as temperatures dipped to fifteen below zero, the family got worried and put him in their cellar, where he would fly around, talk, and play games, according to Bureau.

But one day, he pecked open a bag of ready cement and ingested some and died. The family was devastated, Bureau recalled.

"I was really bent. I didn't realize I could be so attached to a crow. It was sad—it really was."

Smokey was featured in the *Morning Sentinel* several times. A photo with his front-page obituary shows then-Police Officer Joe Plisga directing traffic on Main Street downtown as Smokey struts across the street.

"There's people that remember him to this day," Bureau said. "They see me and say, 'Aren't you the guy that had that crow?' So many people have their own stories about him. He was absolutely amazing. Crows are so smart. You wouldn't believe the things that Smokey would do—carry a twig a long ways and hop up on the table to give it to me when I was doing a project. It was quite remarkable. I had so much fun with that crow."

Recently, Bureau went to Wendy's restaurant on Main Street, and there was a group of crows walking around. He saved some of his hamburger for them, and he looked one right in the eye and talked to it, he recalled.

"I could see my crow," he said. "They're such beautiful birds."
(January 22, 2017)

At Home in Waterville

Harold LaBrie came walking down Temple Street in Waterville, hauling a metal wagon piled high with crates and bags of beer bottles. He swung a left into the parking lot of Damon's Beverage on Front Street, parked the cart by the bottle redemption door, and carried the crates and bags into the shop one by one.

"A lot of people do different things. I collect bottles and buy cat food for my cats," he said. "I have two white ones."

LaBrie, sixty-nine, stood at the counter while employee Bobby Frappier plucked the large empty brown bottles of Natural Ice beer out of the crates. LaBrie said he gets five cents apiece for them. A wiry man with a gray beard and wearing dark tinted bifocals, a camouflage cap, blue work pants, and a bright blaze-orange sweatshirt, LaBrie was friendly when I approached him to talk.

"If you get liquor bottles, it's fifteen cents," he said. "I come here sometimes twice a month, sometimes once a month. I live in a room on Elm Street."

He said a friend gives him the bottles, and he uses the money to buy food for Rose, his ten-year-old pure white, part Siamese cat, and Rose's eight-year-old son, Punk.

"I used to haul the cart with my bike, but somebody stole the bike last year," he said. "I paid about one hundred and eighty dollars for it. I bought it at a pawn shop. A guy borrowed it and said he was going to put it back, and he never did. It was yellow and gold, and it had a rack in the back."

LaBrie walked over to the liquor store side of Damon's where he collected $17.25 for the bottles—a pretty good haul, he agreed. We went outside and stood in the busy lot, where people were coming and going, and chatted some more about LaBrie's life. He was born at the former Sisters Hospital, now Mount St. Joseph Nursing Home, on College Avenue, one of ten children. They lived on Water Street in the South End early on. His father worked in the woods, and his mother was a waitress at the Bob-In on Temple Street. The family moved around the city when he was young and for a time lived at Head of Falls across Front Street from Damon's, which formerly was called Jokas' Discount Beverage.

"The Wyandotte mill was there, and the toll bridge used to cost two cents, and then it went to five cents. There were a lot of houses, and we had a good time. I walked to school on Myrtle Street. Now everything's changed."

He worked at various places over the years, including in the laundry room at then-Thayer Hospital where he also did housekeeping and cleaned the operating room.

"Then I worked at the Bob-In. I was cleaning up and bouncing a little bit. I worked in a chicken barn in Winslow and at Ralston Purina. I've been moving around. Why sit in one place?"

LaBrie was employed at the former John Martin's Manor as head dishwasher and did cleaning as well until the place closed a few years ago. He was married and divorced twice but never had any children. He said he used to be a drinker but stopped in 1997 when he was diagnosed with diabetes after blacking out and being hit by a car.

Now, he does odd jobs, cutting grass and weed-whacking for churches and other places. He used to haul his lawnmower on the wagon behind his bike, but when his bike was stolen, he had to haul the wagon by hand. As we chatted, Frappier, the man who works the counter in the bottle redemption shop, came outside and approached LaBrie.

"Somebody stole your bike, you said? Can you use a mountain bike? Because I have a mountain bike at my house. We bought the house, and there were two bikes there, and nobody wanted them. I gave one to my sister, and the other one needs a tire. I believe a twenty-four-inch."

With that, LaBrie perked up and said he sure could use the bike and he has tires, including one that would fit.

"I'll bring it down then," Frappier said. "It'll be here tomorrow."

LaBrie was happy and grateful for the offer and said it will make his job a lot easier.

"People say, 'You're always around,' and I say, 'I'm everywhere.' That's why I tell people walking and riding a bike is good, and they ask why. Well, I say, you might lose a little weight. I'm not trying to criticize you. I walk, and I'm sixty-nine years old."

LaBrie seems real happy, and I ask why that is.

"I'm my own boss, I do what I want, and I like my work," he said. "I got no complaint. I like Waterville. I was born in Waterville, and I know a lot of places. I used to go to the Boys Club when I was a young kid."

We went inside the bottle shop to say goodbye to Frappier and get a photo of him with LaBrie. Employee Dawn Braley, fifty-five, said she was not surprised Frappier offered to give LaBrie a bike.

"That's Bobby—that's how he is," she said. "He has a big heart, and customers come in short a few nickels, and he gives it to them. He's good to all the customers." (April 16, 2018)

Farewell to Peter Michaud

Peter Michaud was one of those people you weren't afraid of once you got to know him.

He'd walk around downtown Waterville with a bayonet at his side, wearing a wide-brimmed hat and tall boots and pulling a wagon with two or three kerosene cans inside, along with groceries and other necessities.

He lived off College Avenue behind the car wash in a grove of trees that served as his outdoor home, where he wore paths in the grass that meandered through the complex. His belongings included a small tent where he slept summer and winter, piles of blankets and sleeping bags, a few clothes, some pots and pans he hung from tree branches, and a chair or two.

Peter had chickens perched in the trees around his compound. He gave them French names and called to them as he led me on a tour one summer day while I was writing a story about him. They laid a lot of eggs, and Peter would give away the ones he couldn't eat himself. He liked fresh eggs, but he loved his chickens more.

Often, you'd see him walking down College Avenue, back erect, waving to cars. Whenever he turned to the east, he bowed as if he were meeting the queen. Most people who lived in Waterville knew him, although visitors eyed him suspiciously, and sometimes the uninformed would call the police to report a middle-aged man with a sword heading toward downtown. That was many years ago, when the police department was in the basement of City Hall and had an entrance off Front Street across from the *Morning Sentinel* office near Head of Falls.

I often met Peter as I sat on the bench in the hallway of the police department early mornings, waiting for an officer to deliver the police log from the night before so I could copy down the complaints. The bench and communications center where the dispatchers worked were a couple of steps down from street level. Peter would open the heavy door off Front Street, descend the steps, bow to the dispatchers behind the glass window, and ask for Chief John Morris.

When Morris appeared, Peter would salute and say, "Permission to come aboard, sir." Morris would reply, "Permission granted" and emerge from the locked door to greet him.

Morris, who now is the state commissioner of public safety, and Michaud were retired US Navy men and respected and understood each other. When Peter faced challenges from people who misunderstood or were afraid of him, Morris would intervene. He was a police chief who believed in community policing, getting to know the people he served, and, especially, befriending and looking out for those who were "different."

An education expert told me many years ago that one cannot teach effectively without knowing his students—their backgrounds, histories, interests, strengths, shortcomings, and the like, and I think Morris understood that concept well and used it successfully in many cases that required de-escalation.

Peter infrequently would address the City Council about an issue of concern, and sometimes he'd get agitated and raise his voice. All it would take to calm him was for Morris to approach the podium and stand with him.

Peter was lucky to have had a landowner who allowed him to live the way he did for a long time and, I've heard, even offered to build him a house, but Peter didn't want to be confined by four walls. He loved the outdoors. But the time came when he was asked to leave the property, and he did, albeit reluctantly. He moved to Augusta for a while and then to a homeless veterans shelter in Boston.

From there, he wrote letters to let me know he was OK, and then he moved to Canada to another veterans home and continued to write, though his letters eventually stopped, and we lost touch. I often wondered what happened to him.

When an obituary appeared recently in our newspaper for Peter Arthur Michaud, I did a double-take. Could it be the same Peter Michaud I knew in Waterville so many years ago?

The dateline was Leamington, Ontario, Canada, and the young, dark-haired, bearded and mustached man wearing a checkered shirt and smiling in the photo was surely him, many years before he came to live in the trees off College Avenue.

He had died April 27 at seventy-two after finding his peace, living in Ontario for the last nine years of his life, the obituary said.

He graduated from Waterville High School in 1964, attended Southern Maine Technical Institute, and earned a two-year degree that certified him as a machinist, according to the obituary. He then enlisted in the US Navy and served more than four years during

Vietnam on the ship the USS Hector. During his time in the Navy, he earned a National Defense Service Medal, a letter of commendation, and the Vietnam Service Medal with a Bronze Star. Later, he earned a degree in mechanical engineering from University of Maine at Orono.

I searched the obituary to try to find some clue as to why he might have abandoned the traditional life for the one he chose and could find only one. "Peter's life was not without tribulations. He did his best to surmount his challenges."

I sensed that he was loved, this man who seemed alone in the world but whose obituary said he was survived by four sisters and several nieces and nephews. I was comforted in knowing he had family who cared. And it's clear they understood his wishes in the directive, "In lieu of flowers, please support your local veterans' services."

Once a regular figure in downtown Waterville, Peter disappeared one day, never to return, but he is part of the fabric of this city we call home, a thread in the stories we carry around with us and pass on, some surviving through time and others dissipating like a summer rainstorm that arrives in a rush and thins away, slowly, to vapor. I have a feeling Peter's presence will be felt downtown for a long time by those who remember him.

As summer nears its end, I see him clearly in my mind's eye, marching east on Common Street by Castonguay Square, bayonet swaying from his hip, gold tooth gleaming. He halts at Front Street to salute, bows to the east, and continues north to the police station. He served his country well, something for which he was proud and spoke of often during his life.

Now we may salute and bow to him in his death.

(September 10, 2018)

"Parting is Such Sweet Sorrow"

Emily Rowden Fournier was as memorable a character as I had ever met in my career. She was colorful, smart, generous, and had an imagination that was just out of this world.

Fournier, of Fairfield, died a week ago in a tragic whitewater rafting accident, at thirty-two. But in her short time on this Earth, she lived life with more joy, passion, and verve than many of us will ever achieve. She loved theater, literature, and history and was environmentally conscious. She advocated for the underdog.

I met Fournier in 2014 when she told me about her plans to throw a 450th birthday bash for William Shakespeare, the English playwright, poet, and actor. She was twenty-six at the time, and I was amazed by her love of Shakespeare and knowledge of his works. She had read all his plays and poems dozens of times and memorized lines from many.

"My favorite sonnet is 'Sonnet 130,' which starts, 'My mistress's eyes are nothing like the sun,'" she told me.

At the time, Fournier and her family were establishing the Recycled Shakespeare Company, a theater troupe that would perform Shakespeare's plays using mostly recycled materials for costumes, sets, and props. She was about to launch auditions for *A Midsummer Night's Dream*.

"We are going to try to cast everyone who auditions," Fournier said. "If one hundred and fifty people audition, then we're going to have one hundred and forty fairies. We really just want everyone to be involved. Our whole concept is to create fun and enthusiastic productions utilizing recycled and repurposed materials and the local talent that is here. That's the important piece of local theater—enthusiasm. We're not asking people to be Broadway performers."

That was the way Fournier was—warm, welcoming, and inclusive of everyone who wanted to learn about Shakespeare and theater itself. She just beamed when talking about it. She had an almost jubilant outlook on theater and on life itself. I remember thinking while listening to her speak that here's this grown woman who never lost the imagination she honed in childhood.

She recalled her mother, Lyn Rowden, taking her to see *Macbeth* at Colby College when she was a little girl.

"I think I was the youngest person in the audience by about fifteen years," she said. "I started reading Shakespeare when I was in kindergarten—I'm not joking. I saw the play *Hamlet* when I was in kindergarten, and I went home and took out my Mom's Shakespeare book, and I read *Hamlet* and memorized the 'Goodnight, sweet prince' monologue. I performed it to my mother with a teddy bear."

She would later go on to teach adult classes out of her home about Shakespearean literature and Shakespeare, and she was only in her twenties. She had grown up in Fairfield and attended Lawrence High School briefly before enrolling in the Maine School of Science and Mathematics in Limestone, from which she graduated in 2006. While in high school, she wrote an in-depth piece on Shakespeare's view of feminism, according to female roles in *Romeo and Juliet*—focusing on the characters of Juliet, the nurse, and Juliet's mother.

"I also focused on how that pertained to the Elizabethan times and the censorship of literature and productions," she said.

She attended St. Anselm College in Manchester, New Hampshire, where she majored in English specifically because of her love of Shakespeare. She received a bachelor's degree in 2011.

The thing Fournier loved about Shakespeare, she said, is that his works are universal. Written in the late 1500s and early 1600s, they explore what it is to be human, and that is something all humans are trying to find answers to, she told me.

"His works are not just set in a time—they span all time. He can move anyone to tears. We can still feel the pain that is felt in *Romeo and Juliet* or understand why Titus Andronicus grieves so much over the rape of his daughter. We watch HBO for the same sensation."

On Shakespeare's 450th birthday in 2014—he was allegedly born around April 23, 1564, in Stratford-upon-Avon—Fournier, her husband Joshua, her mother, and friends donned elaborate Elizabethan costumes and paraded through downtown Waterville, waving sticks with green and red ribbons and singing songs written by Shakespeare. Her husband was dressed as the bard himself and her mother as Queen Elizabeth I. Because I planned to write a story about the event, I tagged along with them. It was one of the more fun assignments I've undertaken.

"Anon!" Fournier called to a woman who poked her head out of a storefront door. "Happy 450th birthday to the great William Shakespeare!"

Fournier was wearing a pouffy, multicolored dress with strings tightly tied at the waist and curtsied to those she met. She and the others read aloud sonnets as they poked their heads into businesses and sang "Happy Birthday" to the delight of spectators. She led the troupe to Selah Tea Cafe downtown where she had organized a reading of Shakespeare's 154 sonnets and had talked many people, including myself, into reading aloud a sonnet.

Two years later, our paths crossed again when Fournier's friend Valerie Tieman was murdered in Fairfield. Fournier had gotten Tieman involved in the theater troupe, and they acted onstage together. Wrought with grief over her death, Fournier insisted on commenting for a story I was writing, as she wanted the world to know what a sweet and loving person Tieman was.

Also that year, I ran into Fournier and her husband at the Fairfield Historical Society's Christmas open house where they were dressed in Civil War-era costumes and giving tours of the history house. I learned she had been a volunteer there since she was in junior high school, as she loved history.

She never ceased to amaze me with her zest for life and her love of family and of the activities in which she took part. When I learned that she also was a whitewater rafter, I was not surprised. I imagine her now, minutes before her death, happy, joyful, and reveling in the river ride, that lovely face of hers beaming in the sun. It was her final act before the curtain went down on an extraordinary life well lived.

We, your fans, shall miss you, dear Emily. Parting is such sweet sorrow. But methinks we shall meet again.

Anon! (July 17, 2020)

Bucket List

Viviane Fotter is one of the strongest women I have ever known.

She worked in the Diamond Match factory in Oakland for thirty-four years while raising six boys, has had more surgeries than you can count, suffers from rheumatoid arthritis and other serious health problems, and never complains. She's always smiling.

Viviane, who will be ninety-one in January, is now in hospice care and living in Benton with her son Steve and his wife, Linda. She left her waterfront home in the Belgrade Lakes because she needed more round-the-clock care. Viviane is in a wheelchair, on oxygen, and fragile, but that doesn't stop her from chasing adventure.

"She's working on her bucket list," Steve told me this week. "We got her in the pool last summer. She was with the grandchildren, and they were splashing each other. She wanted to go down in the basement to see my trains, so we carried her down the stairs in the wheelchair, and she loved it. She stayed for about an hour."

Steve had called to invite me to share in another of his mother's bucket list forays. I was honored to be invited to such a momentous occasion, which I will tell you about in a moment.

But first, I must relate that Viviane and I go a long way back. I met her twenty-seven years ago when we were hospital roommates, and we have kept in touch through Christmas cards ever since. She had back surgery requiring her to lie flat on her back. I had intestinal issues and could not eat. We were both in rough shape, but we lifted

Viviane Fotter, 90, meets Taylor for the first time before her birthday ride. Her grandson Joe Fotter helps her. Photo by Michael G. Seamans | *Morning Sentinel.*

each other's spirits by talking and telling stories long into the night when we couldn't sleep.

On Mother's Day that year, 1993, Steve came to see her in the hospital, armed with his guitar, and sang to her. It was the sweetest thing. Steve is a guitar teacher and performer and loves his mother fiercely. In January, he hosted a big ninetieth birthday party for her at a Waterville restaurant attended by dozens of friends and family. There was a nice lunch, a big cake, stories told, and lots of laughter; of course, Steve sang her favorite songs.

But back to Viviane's bucket list.

"A month ago, Mom blurted out of the blue, 'I've never been on a horse,'" Steve told me. "I had no idea it was on her bucket list. I've been with my Mom sixty-five years, and I didn't know that."

Steve vowed to grant her wish. On Wednesday, a warm, sunny fall day, I drove out to Steve and Linda's house where their nephew Joe Fotter helped get Viviane into the car to head to Silver Lining Acres, a horse farm a few miles away in Clinton owned by Joe's stepdaughter, Kyrstie Tracy. Before leaving, Steve presented his mother with a pretty chocolate cake with orange, yellow, and white frosting and topped with a plastic horse. On the cake was written the words, "Congrats, Mom."

You see, Viviane was about to ride a horse for the first time in her life—a lifelong dream since growing up in Waterville, one of nine children, she told me.

"I think I've done most everything I wanted to do," she said. "But the horse…When I was about ten or twelve, growing up in Waterville, we went to a farm. It was about apple time, and these people had horses, and when I saw that horse, I thought he was beautiful, and I thought someday I might be able to ride. I've mentioned it as the years go by. Then Kyrstie got her horses and I thought, 'Gee, I'd like to go and have a ride around that arena.'"

We all drove to the horse farm where Steve's friends Mike Schimpff and Alan Getchell and Getchell's daughter, Ellie, age eight, were waiting to help. Kyrstie also was there with Taylor, an easy-going, twelve-year-old Appaloosa. A Fotter family friend, Monica Charette, was ready with a video camera.

Steve presented his mother with a bouquet of red roses and baby's breath, and the action began.

The men loaded Viviane in her wheelchair onto the bed of a pickup truck, which then was backed up to the horse. Joe climbed onto its back, behind the saddle. Viviane was lifted onto the saddle, sideways.

With Joe's arm wrapped around his grandmother and Kyrstie leading the horse, they entered the arena and circled it several times. Kyrstie's four-year-old black English lab, Duke, followed along. Playing his guitar, Steve sang, "Happy trails to you, until we meet again…" as he strolled with the group.

Viviane, donning a brown cowboy hat, was beaming.

"Giddy up there, girl," she said to the horse. "You're a good girl."

It was a joyful several minutes, and, as all good things must come to an end, the entourage eventually headed back to the gate. Viviane thanked everyone, and they all clapped. I asked her what she thought of her ride.

"For the record," she said, "I thought it was wonderful, amazing, and awesome."

She turned to Kyrstie to thank her for helping to knock another item off her bucket list.

"Any time," Kyrstie replied. "Anything for you, Viv."

(October 16, 2020)

Peg

It was around this time a year ago that we visited our friend Peg Clifford in China Village. It would be the next-to-last time we saw her before she died just after Christmas, at ninety-five. It was always a joy to visit her, because she was so engaging, funny, and smart.

She also lived in a big, old house that had been in her family for more than one hundred years and was passed down through the generations with everything in the house staying exactly as it was. The kitchen was ancient but impeccably kept, complete with a black cast iron sink and antique dishes, tables, and chairs—even an old wood cookstove.

Peg wasn't very tall, but she was strong and had short, naturally brown hair, right into her nineties.

Her living room had a large desk, on which sat Peg's rotary phone—she never updated to a push button or cellphone and never owned a television. There was a fireplace and hearth, shelves of books, and tall windows that let in the sun on a cold November day. We'd sit in hard-backed chairs and talk about politics, family, friends, and music.

Ah, yes, music.

Peg was a classical cellist and taught stringed instruments to children in her home, which had a music room complete with an old, upright Steinway piano. Peg and my husband, Phil, were members of a string quartet, and they played together on Fridays for years, except in the summer when everyone was too busy, alternating between the four homes—two in Harpswell, Peg's in China, and ours in Waterville. They would arrive at 10 a.m., play for two hours, stop for lunch, and then sometimes play some more. When they came to our house and if I wasn't working, I had the privilege of hearing them play as I sat in the next room and read or wrote cards. I'd make the main lunch dish, and the three who traveled brought a salad, bread, and dessert.

Peg was an especially good baker and one time brought a terrific pineapple upside-down cake that was so good, I asked her for the recipe afterward. As was often her practice when talking about food or family, she told us a story about the cake.

It turns out the maraschino cherries on top of the pineapple were quite unusual in that they were old—very, very old.

"That bottle of cherries was in the refrigerator when my aunt lived in the house, and she died in 1971," Peg said, grinning. "I've been using them ever since."

Needless to say, while the pineapple upside-down cake was delicious, some of us opted not to consume the half-century-old cherries on top, though those of us who did suffered no ill effects. We sure did have fun laughing about those cherries. To this day, we retell the story as a way to note what an unusual woman Peg was—in so many respects.

Besides having no TV but keeping her rotary phone, Peg was a practical, no-nonsense woman who didn't suffer fools lightly. She read the *Wall Street Journal* every day and subscribed to several magazines, including *The Economist, National Geographic, Time,* and *BBC Music.* She paid no attention to celebrity gossip. Our lunch conversation one day included a brief reference to O.J. Simpson.

"Who's O.J. Simpson?" Peg asked, in earnest.

On our visit to Peg's just before Thanksgiving last year, we gave her the sad news that a well-loved member of the quartet, Louise Huntington, who was eighty-six, had been diagnosed with a terminal illness. Peg's stoic exterior melted away, and she began to cry. It was the first time we had seen her shed a tear. Peg passed away before Louise did, leaving all of us bereft. Because she never married and had no children, the big house in China Village where she lived and died was emptied out and put up for sale, ending a long family legacy.

It's difficult to conceive of the fact that we'll never see Peg or Louise again or visit Peg in her museum of a house that exuded history, tradition, and familial warmth. But in my mind's eye, I see that old place in all its glory, Peg sitting in the living room flanked by newspapers, magazines, and mail, telling a good story.

It's all so vivid, I know I'll never forget any of it, right down to her inimitable, joyful laugh. (November 13, 2020)

Homeless in Waterville

Willis Carlow says living on the streets is no picnic.

"I just want people to understand that it's a very, very tough life to live. I've been homeless three times, and each time, it just gets harder and harder."

I met the twenty-year-old Carlow and his friends, Ana Zinkovitch, nineteen, and her boyfriend, Kevyn Warren, twenty-seven, Wednesday in downtown Waterville after watching them push a grocery cart with all their belongings up the Water Street hill toward town.

They crossed the intersection, approached City Hall, and entered through the health and welfare department door on Front Street.

After a while, they emerged, pushing their cart full of blankets, clothes, a tent—and two small black cats named Shadow and Buddy, housed in a purple pet carrier. They had all slept in the tent in the woods off Water Street on Tuesday night, they said.

"I've been like this for about six months," Carlow said. "It's getting cold now, so I'm trying to get a place."

They had applied for assistance at City Hall but were denied because their income was too high, according to paperwork they produced. Carlow gets Social Security income from being disabled. Warren, who worked at Burger King for two weeks, also is disabled.

"I have a hard time focusing," Warren said. "If I see something on the ground, I stare at it."

The city is working to find them a hotel room, but it might take a couple of days, they said. Warren has been trying to get Zinkovitch and Carlow jobs at Burger King so that they can save up enough money to get an apartment or trailer.

"Ana and I were living on College Avenue," Warren said. "Our rent was eight hundred a month, and the landlord increased it because we had an air-conditioning unit. She put it up to nine hundred, and we couldn't afford it so she kicked us out."

That was Monday, two days before they started staying in the tent with Carlow, a cousin of Zinkovitch.

"I've been living in a tent and camper for about six months in Clinton," Carlow said. "I just came to Waterville because I had more friends out here and more supportive people."

Warren said he and Zinkovitch met about four years ago at a homeless shelter in Skowhegan. They were also homeless before they got the apartment on College Avenue six months ago.

"We were living outside in Bangor," Warren said. "We were camping out behind Shaw's supermarket, in the park. I have no problem with the cold because my body is always hot, but Ana's anemic so she had a hard time. I had to cover her up and cuddle to keep her warm."

Zinkovitch, who grew up in Waterville, is hearing impaired, which makes communicating difficult. She and Warren, of South Paris, are high school graduates; Carlow, a Clinton native, is not.

"I dropped out in the eleventh grade because of bullying," he said. "I haven't had an easy life, but I treat people the way I want to be treated."

The three seemed humble and were affectionate with the cats.

"They're the only thing that we really have left, so it sucks—it really does," Carlow said.

He told me that he, Zinkovitch and Warren would stand by each other.

"We went into this together, we're going to make it out together," he said.

Warren was late for work, and they needed to get something to eat so I said goodbye, but not before asking if they had money for lunch. They assured me that, between Warren and Carlow, they had enough food stamps.

Then the trio trekked north on Front Street, with Zinkovitch toting a knapsack and Warren lugging the cat carrier.

(September 17, 2021)

The Skowhegan Class of 1947

Growing up in Skowhegan during World War II was a time like no other.

Phyllis Chamberlain can attest to that.

"I can remember going on drives, looking for metal—for any piece of scrap metal," she said. "It was for the war effort, to make ships, airplanes, and other equipment."

Chamberlain, ninety-two, was sitting in her sunny Skowhegan kitchen Thursday with three fellow graduates from Skowhegan High School and Bloomfield Academy's Class of 1947. They have been gathering monthly for more than ten years to play cards, share lunch, and reminisce. The group was larger at first but has dwindled over time.

Thursday was St. Patrick's Day, and Chamberlain was cooking up a corned beef and cabbage dinner, with the aroma wafting through the country house as the group talked and laughed and spoke of old times.

Abby Provencher, ninety-one, also recalled people in Skowhegan foraging for scrap metal during the war, when Franklin D. Roosevelt was president.

"If we got anything, we'd bring it down to the Strand Theatre, and we'd see a movie, free," she said. "My grandfather owned a lot behind the Catholic Cemetery, and there was a big iron sink there. I can't remember who helped me, but we walked down to the theater with that big iron sink."

In those days, people mixed up their own margarine, tossing a blob of color in to make it yellow, Babe Lowit recalled. Items were scarce, and people used ration cards to buy things like gasoline, meat, and sugar.

"You always knew a military service person who had extra coupons to get gas," said Lowit, ninety-one, now of Lewiston.

A retired math teacher at Brunswick High School, Billy Cockburn, ninety-two, of Brunswick—and the only man in the group Thursday—was a baseball, basketball, football, and track star in high school. He is the only male still alive from the Class of 1947 and believed to be one of only thirteen class members left, according to Provencher, whose maiden name is Turcotte. Because he is the sole male, Cockburn gets special treatment when he leaves the monthly reunion.

"I get a doggy bag," he said, to laughter from the women.

Having graduated from high school seventy-five years ago, he and the women wanted to show me some of their class memorabilia, which they placed on a table in Chamberlain's sun room. There was a 1947 yearbook called the "Lever," the program from their

Classmates from Skowhegan High School and Bloomfield Academy's Class of 1947. (Clockwise from left): Billy Cockburn, Leona Sinclair, Abby Provencher, Babe Lowitt, and Phyllis Chamberlain. Photo by Rich Abrahamson | *Morning Sentinel*.

graduation on June 13 that year, a booklet commemorating their fiftieth class reunion, and photographs.

Provencher, who lives in the same house in Skowhegan where she grew up, was a cheerleader in school. She brought her black and orange beanie cap and Skowhegan cheerleading letters.

"We wore a black sweater, and the letters were sewn on the front of it," she said.

The high school in 1947 was perched atop a long, slow hill overlooking the Kennebec River. The building is gone now, replaced by housing.

But Chamberlain—whose maiden name is Boynton—Provencher, Lowit, and Cockburn remember the school days well. The girls wore saddle shoes, penny loafers, and plaid "poodle" skirts, named as such because they had a poodle sewn onto the front. Everyone was a friend, students didn't drink, take drugs, or use curse words, and people listened to the radio or went to the movies for entertainment. They recalled only one classmate who owned a car.

"My parents were the first to get a TV," said Lowit, whose maiden name also is Turcotte, though she and Provencher are not related. "Kids would look in our windows to watch it."

Social media was nonexistent. Chamberlain said people now serving in the military may stay in touch with family via social media, but during the war, communication was much different.

"If we heard from my brother once in a few months, it was a miracle, and it was one of those censored letters that came by snail mail. Words were blacked out. We might not hear from him in two or three months, and then we'd get three letters at a time."

Some of their male classmates went off to serve in the war and returned to graduate, they said. The day the war ended in 1945, under Harry Truman's presidency, is forever etched in Provencher's memory. She was ushering a show in the grandstand at the Skowhegan State Fair, and it was announced over the loudspeaker.

"Fire trucks came up and blew their whistles," she said. "It was just such a relief. There was a big, huge celebration during fair week."

Provencher, Lowit, Cockburn, Chamberlain, and her daughter, Leona Sinclair, who has been adopted by the monthly group, said they want to hold a seventy-fifth class reunion in June at Chamberlain's home.

"We're in our nineties," she said. "We don't mind looking it, but we hate to act it." (March 18, 2022)

A Little Spot of Heaven

Peter Gregory's little slice of heaven is the small, grassy spot just outside his apartment door, at the corner of Summer and Gold streets in Waterville's South End. There, he built a sort of cage several years ago, using metal stakes, chicken wire, and lots of zip ties. The cage is about ten feet tall, and inside it are several thirteen-foot towering cherry tomato plants growing in large pots.

"They'll grow until the first frost," Gregory said. "I just keep them watered every day. I've got two thousand tomatoes already this year. Every year I get more and more as long as I keep the squirrels out."

Gregory, fifty-eight, tends his plants every day and says his secret is feeding them Miracle-Gro once a week. He also tends to a towering mass of morning glories in the shape of a Christmas tree beside his porch steps. Several small pots of peppermint, which he uses to make tea, hang from his porch. He loves the scent of peppermint.

A tall, slim man with straight red hair and hazel eyes, Gregory seems happy and upbeat, despite his physical ailments. He suffers from dystonia and tardive dyskinesia, nerve and muscle conditions that make it difficult to walk and stay balanced. He moves carefully, holding on to a Hannaford grocery cart he keeps parked next to the porch. A few years ago when he was in bad shape, his physical therapist would have him do a certain number of leg and arm exercises, but he got so tired of being immobile that he insisted on doing twice that amount. He worked hard at it and eventually got back on his feet.

Gregory refuses to stay idle. About three times a week, he pushes the shopping cart to Hannaford on Kennedy Memorial Drive more than a mile away, leaning on it to maintain balance. Hannaford officials were kind to him and gave him the cart, he said. When it gets old and wobbly, they replace it with a new one.

Peter Gregory harvests tomatoes. Photo by Rich Abrahamson | *Morning Sentinel.*

"If I leave here at nine o'clock in the morning, I'll get there, probably at eleven," he said. "It takes about an hour to shop and then another two hours to get back home. I don't use the sidewalk because it's too uneven. I stay on the side of the road."

He keeps more than a dozen milk jugs filled with water on his porch steps to water his plants, which sometimes include larger tomatoes and peppers. He acknowledges his planting method is a bit different than most people's, as he doesn't start with seeds or seedlings. Instead, he buys a handful of cherry tomatoes or a whole beefsteak tomato, breaks them apart, removes the seeds, and plants them right into his soil. They sprout up in about two weeks, he said.

"I usually cook some of them; we eat them in salads, boil them down, and freeze them or bake them in oil. One tomato can have a hundred seeds, so I really don't have to buy many at all."

He caught the planting bug from his grandmother while growing up in New Britain, Connecticut. He helped her plant and pick strawberries and loved it.

His family, including a sister and two brothers, moved to Waterville when he was a high school freshman. He earned a letter in cross country and track, of which he was very proud. When he developed health problems and could no longer run, they made him a manager.

His was an abusive upbringing, as his mother would beat him regularly, he said.

"She never paid the bills. We starved a lot. We never had much food. At the high school, they let me come in the kitchen and work, and they gave me extra food."

The family moved back to Connecticut when Gregory was seventeen, and he got a job in the high school kitchen, for which he received food and a regular paycheck that his mother took from him.

"She beat me to get that check, and I had to give it to her. One day, I called the police, and a cop said, 'You are old enough to get out.' So I left. A neighbor took me in. After that, I rode my ten-speed bike up here to Waterville. It took me three days. I left on a Friday, and I got up here on a Sunday night."

He stayed with a friend on Moor Street in the South End, got a job dishwashing at The Manor, a restaurant on College Avenue, found an apartment and met his would-be wife, Margaret, whom he has been with for thirty-one years.

During our visit Monday, Gregory said he collects pumpkin and squash seeds to feed the crows and blue jays that visit his lawn. He motioned to a squirrel scurrying around on a nearby patch of grass and told me he keeps a bucket of peanuts for it.

"She can't focus very well, because she can't see a lot," he said. "I call her One Eye. I feed her all winter long." (November 11, 2022)

Never a Bad Day
on the Kennebec River

It's always a good day on the river—that's Willie Grenier's philosophy, anyway.

Whether he catches shad or not, the seventy-five-year-old Waterville resident and avid fisherman enjoys being on the Kennebec River in his 1999, fourteen-foot aluminum Lund for which he bought a new fifteen-horsepower Mercury motor this year. His left hand on the tiller, Grenier motored out into the river Thursday morning from the boat landing at the south end of Water Street in Waterville, the sun at full tilt, not a cloud in the sky.

It was sixty-three degrees and quiet except for birds chattering and the sound of water lapping against the sides of the boat. About one hundred yards to the south, cars and trucks on the Donald V. Carter Memorial Bridge looked like toys moving along, high up over the river. About three-quarters of a mile to the north, the Lockwood Dam jutted out into the water.

We cruised along to the Winslow side of the river. As we approached Fort Halifax Park at the confluence of the Sebasticook and Kennebec rivers, Grenier waved to a fisherman who was standing, thigh-high, in the water, casting a fly.

"Do you know him?" I asked.

"Everybody's a friend," Grenier said. "I have a lot of friends who fish over there. They put up with me."

Having fished since he was five, Grenier knows a lot about not only fishing but also river ecology. A retired, thirty-five-year Clinton Elementary School teacher, he has taught river ecology to many high school and college students over the years and, for ten years, worked with Project Healing Waters, taking disabled veterans out to fish. A member of Trout Unlimited, he taught at that organization's Maine Trout Camp in Solon.

Standing in the boat, Grenier raised his rod and cast a fly off to the east. An osprey flew overhead. The river level was a bit too low Thursday to fish in Ticonic Bay, the area between Fort Halifax Park and the Lockwood Dam where the alewife population exploded after the Edwards Dam in Augusta was removed in 1999. It is where Grenier typically fishes for shad, as it is a world-class shad fishing spot, but we stayed a bit downstream.

Soon he got a hit—a sixteen-inch, silvery gray shad that flopped about in the water until he scooped it up in a net and then slipped it back into the water. He estimated the fish at two pounds and about four years old. Shad born in this part of the river come back here every spring to spawn and then head back to the ocean, sixty-four miles away, he explained. Alewives also are sea-run fish that come up the river to spawn.

The river wasn't always rife with shad, alewives, small and large-mouthed bass, and other fish, but after the passage of the Clean Water Act in 1972, spearheaded by then-Maine Sen. Edmund Muskie, the river ecology improved. Grenier remembers growing up in Lewiston and, at twelve, casting a line in the foul-smelling Androscoggin River while hearing a toilet flush into the river nearby. It was the same situation here in Waterville, where sewage was piped right into the Kennebec.

Maintaining a healthy ecosystem and ensuring Atlantic salmon and other fish have passage upriver so they can spawn and not become extinct is critical, according to Grenier.

"I want to see this river be useful for the next generations," he said. "I'm always looking for the future. I remember as a kid thinking that life would never be good. There was so much pollution. Seeing soot on the top of my father's car, being behind a truck spreading DDT on elm trees and the paint peeling off the car because of it. What they found out later on the Dutch elm disease is that it could be taken care of by putting ladybugs on them, which would have

Willie Grenier on the Kennebec. Photo by Rich Abrahamson | *Morning Sentinel.*

eaten the parasites. Nature has a way of saving itself, and man has a way of destroying it."

An immature eagle soared overhead, near a bald eagle perched in a maple tree on the riverbank. As we headed back to the boat landing, Grenier reflected on his long love of the outdoors.

"To me, fishing was always part of my escape. I thoroughly enjoyed it. It was relief from everyday life. It was my outlet, growing up. It's very peaceful. You never know what you're going to catch."

The most majestic fish to see in the Kennebec is sturgeon, he said.

"I have had a sturgeon jump completely out of the water and splash me in my boat. They're about six feet long."

This summer, Grenier plans to head to Grand Falls on the Dead River, past West Forks, where he camps out of his pickup truck and spends time fishing and reading.

"That is my absolutely favorite place to be," he said.

(May 13, 2022)

EPILOGUE

My father in 2005.

Dear Dad

Dear Dad,

This is going to be a hard letter to write, as it is my last one to you.

But I wanted you to know that you were the best father I ever could have asked for.

Did you hear me tell you that, as I sat by your hospital bedside a week ago? You were sleeping peacefully, but they said you could hear everything I said.

"I love you, Dad," I whispered. "You are the best dad in the whole world."

You raised your eyebrows, and I think that may have been your acknowledgment that you heard. I hope you did. If not, then do you remember what we talked about, the last day we really spoke?

You were lying in your bed at home, holding my mother's hand, and I was leaving for the night. You wondered aloud if you had done enough for us during your long life.

"Are you kidding, Dad?" I said. "How many kids had such a wonderful field and woods to roam in, a vegetable garden, Sunday dinner every week with the family, and parents who stayed together for sixty-four years?"

"You taught us about art, music, literature, politics, and so much more. We were very lucky."

You were smiling then, and I knew all was OK. That is the vision of you I will carry for a long, long time. That, and you in the hospital those last two days, sleeping comfortably, finally out of pain.

I will never hear your voice again, see your smile, hear your stories. My phone will never ring as it did most evenings, with your voice on the other end of the line saying "Well, what's the news today?"

"Pretty good, Dad, how was your day?"

"Oh, I can't complain" (even though you might've had a rough one).

We won't be able to go to the ocean together again or to Montreal, and I won't be able to watch you paint by that perfect light from the north.

But, Dad, we have your beautiful watercolors and oil paintings all around, wrapping us in your warmth and intellect.

When I hear "The Messiah" and see *The Nutcracker* at Christmas, I'll think of you. When I see a horse canter across a field at sunset, I'll sense you there.

On Monday, as your casket lay on a snowy hill in Canaan, draped with red and white roses from Mom and us, I thought about how you would appreciate the simple beauty there.

You loved snowstorms, so it was fitting that you left in a dramatic flurry, the snow and howling wind whipping at our backs.

The mystery of death was present then, as it is now.

Where did you go, and where are you now?

"Is Dad really in that box?" I asked Jane as we stood there, sisters—the youngest in a brood of seven.

"Yes," she said, then paused. "No, it's just his physical body. He's on the ladder, climbing up to the sky, just like in his painting."

She was referring to your oil painting that hangs in the kitchen above the cupboards, near the cellar door. In it, a rope ladder emerges from a snow-covered hill, winding its way through an azure sky to oversized stars that look like snowflakes.

I prefer to think you are at your destination now, free of mortal pain and angst.

Maybe you are our angel now? I know there are certain things you can't do, like take away the ache in our hearts. But I do have a favor to ask, now that you are in the company of the big guy and likely have his ear.

Is there something he can do about getting us a hospice house here in central Maine—a place where dying people can spend their final days surrounded by family and those trained to provide support and comfort to both, around the clock?

We were lucky to have a large family that could take shifts while you were at home, a nursing home that worked wonders, exceptional hospice nurses, and at the end, a hospital staff beyond compare.

But there has to be a simpler, less exhausting, and stressful way to care for people like you, who taught us everything we know, put your life on the line in World War II, and deserved so much more in the end.

I asked the nurse the day before you died why we do not have a hospice house here, like they do in larger cities. Is it a lack of money?

"Yes," said this hospice worker, who does the best she can, rushing from the home of one dying person to the next.

Dad, is there any way you could help coax some philanthropists into helping start a hospice house? I think a lot of people would come on board. After all, the most important thing we have is each other, and we really, really need to do better in this regard.

Meanwhile, Dad, I'm keeping you in my heart and trying to look forward to Christmas, which you loved. It's not easy, but I know it's what you'd want. (December 11, 2010)

Acknowledgments

I thank my late parents, Edwin and Frances Calder, who were great role models for how to live life: with joy, verve, and, always, intellectual curiosity. My older siblings Jane, Laura, Matthew, David, Katherine and Richard filled our home with hijinks, adventure, imagination, and laughter, all of which informed my love for telling a good story.

I thank teachers Christopher Glenn and Muriel Dubuc, post-humously. They inspired, encouraged, and motivated me. Kim Wheeler and Otis Fuller, Nick and Barbara Carbone, Karol and John Youney, and Meneely Townsend, you have been my lifelong ports in the storm.

Thank you, Lisa DeSisto, CEO and publisher of MaineToday Media/Masthead Maine, for supporting my book efforts and for championing all your employees. My appreciation also goes to Scott Monroe, managing editor of the *Morning Sentinel* and *Kennebec Journal*, always a steady hand at the helm. To community news editor Stacy Blanchet, longtime colleague and friend, your advice over the years has been consistently spot on.

To my husband Phil, for always being forgiving when I vow to be home for dinner at six, but don't make it until ten, thank you. Only a former journalist can truly understand that breaking news takes priority every time.

I want to thank editor-in-chief Dean Lunt and the good people at Islandport Press for their generosity, accessibility, and diligence.

And last but not least, thank you to newspaper readers, every-where, for helping to keep our important industry alive.

Photo by Madeline St. Amour.

About the Author

Amy Calder is an award-winning newspaper reporter and columnist for the *Morning Sentinel*, based in Waterville, Maine, where she covers city government and everything from murders and car crashes to fires and drug busts. Her thirty-four-year career started at the *Sentinel's* Somerset County Bureau in Skowhegan, where she served as bureau chief several years and chased stories from Jackman to Fairfield and Farmington to Newport.

Besides covering the news, Calder writes a weekly human interest column, "Reporting Aside," which appears in both the *Sentinel* and *Kennebec Journal*. This book represents a collection of essays based on those columns, which include sketches of the colorful characters and quirky animals she has encountered, as well as personal stories about growing up in rural Skowhegan.

Calder lives in Waterville with her husband, Philip Norvish, and their two cats, Thurston and Bitsy.